CM0074159I

Olli Grau

for Ingrid

Published by:

© 2004 La Ola Verlag bei Blue and White GmbH
Eichenstr. 3, 83083 Riedering, Germany
www.kajak.de

Title of the original German edition:
BESSER WILDWASSERFAHREN by Olli Grau
ISBN 3-9809314-0-1
© 2004 by La Ola Verlag

Author: Olli Grau
Translation: Peter Musch/Cameron Paul
Layout: Jan Haluszka
Photography: Jens Klatt
Additional photography: Manuel Arnu, Olli Grau
Sebastian Gründler, Michael Neumann
Cover: Phillis Arnu on the Soca river, Slovenia.
Cover photo: Manuel Arnu

ISBN 3-9809315-1-X

Olli Grau

White Water Kayaking

The new school of modern white water kayaking

With images by Jens Klatt

 La Ola Verlag

Content

Prologue

Kayaking in white water today is all about fun, enthusiasm for adventure and the experience of nature. As a trend and extreme sport it is attractive and popular, especially among younger people. White water river running has been progressing continuously throughout the last couple of decades, and in some phases the developments have been revolutionary.

Material and equipment such as boats and paddles, specific white water clothing and safety equipment have been continuously developed to the highest standards and most modern designs. Newly refined paddling techniques have evolved and become easier to master in combination with the optimized equipment.

Excellent kayaking schools that employ sophisticated teaching methods offer courses and clinics that speed up learning, and make the sport much more accessible. Today you learn the Eskimo roll in one day!

Today's top athletes on the world kayaking scene perform in spheres and regions that were considered impossible only a few years ago. The technical abilities of today's intermediate kayaker are already greater than standards ever reached in the past. Many upcoming paddlers come to run difficult white water much sooner than decades ago. But even today it is still a long road to becoming an expert who can run a demanding cataract playfully, with ease and safety. Despite improved active safety as a result of these generally higher standards of technical ability, and the subsequent lower number of accidents on the river, safety and rescue technique in white water remains a fundamental issue today.

Today's generation of young white water river runners prefers a relaxed approach to the material, a clear comprehensible book with spectacular photography, straightforward explanatory graphics and a meaningful but manageable text.
Modern techniques, a new style, a new consciousness on the river, together with seriousness and respect. This is what Olli Grau, one of the world's leading alpine extremists, offers with his new school of modern white water kayaking.

It is fun to read, gets greater results in learning and practice and – most importantly – it will bring you endless fun and joy kayaking in white water.

Markus Schmid

8

Andy Phillips, San Giovanni, Piemont, Italien

Introduction

White water paddling is a fascinating sport that literally carries you away. Paddling down a raging river in a kayak is a great natural experience and adventure. On a river you are a discoverer, your curiosity and the current sweep you along and captivate you. Paddling a new section of a river is a challenge, and heading for new frontiers demands a lot of courage. What awaits you around the next bend of the river? A river landscape is mostly an untouched, natural environment in which you often have to solve all manner of alpine problems, and where you can bond with nature and the elements. This can bring the purest experience of joy and total happiness. The greater your skill and knowledge of white water paddling, the more likely you will triumph on even the most demanding rivers.

Good technique is a basic prerequisite for a white water paddler, because white water paddling confronts you with constantly changing conditions. There is no such thing as mundane repeats of the same movement – you continually have to find new combinations of your standard maneuvers and techniques.

On a river you are your own master. Unlike in our over-regulated society, on the river you are free to, or sometimes even have to, find and choose your own way and your own tactic.

Next to strategy, social competence is also required. Even though white water paddling is an individual sport, it is normally carried out in groups. You have friends to share with – mostly fun and joy, sometimes also danger and fear. And this team work, as well as the group dynamics, shape your character and bring enormous reward.

So what is the "new school of kayaking" all about?

In the early years of white water paddling, classic paddlers simply crashed down rivers and cataracts - no guts, no glory! No wonder! The boats were very long and heavy, hard to maneuver, and paddling technique was still in its infancy. The only thing that counted was: full steam ahead!

Not until the eighties and the nineties, when paddlers orientated themselves towards the skills and techniques of slalom paddling, did a more active and athletic style of paddling begin to evolve. Paddlers aimed for more control, more technique and, last but not least, more fun. People started to paddle more analytically and less emotionally, with more skill and less fear.

The changes resulting from this mind-shift were the basis for a development of a new direction in modern paddle sports. Boats and gear were radically improved. In particular the shorter hull shapes with flat bottoms boosted a new style of athletic and dynamic paddling, which also helped to make white water paddling safer and more predictable. New possibilities offered themselves and the limits were pushed to incredible heights. But not only the high end and hard core side of paddling profited from this development. Leisure paddlers are also now working at a level nobody thought possible only twenty years ago. The victory of stress-free paddling has given a new image to paddle sports – no more heroes, just fun loving people savoring the most basic of elements. Not only are you no longer paddling for reputation, but you're paddling with more control - for the pure fun of it!

That's what this book is all about.

Thanks

Just like paddling, the success of such a book depends on the help of many helping hands. The same goes for the river – you are pretty alone without your friends and buddies.

First of all I want to thank my publisher Hans Mayer. He inspired and motivated me for years with this project. Without him, I figure I'd still be sitting in front of a blank piece of paper.

With his essays in this book, Markus Schmid has proved himself not only to be a practical expert on white water sports, but also a profound thinker and connoisseur of white water literature. His passionate work in all the other parts of the book also gives it a special something, I think.

Thanks to:

Jan Haluszka for his solid work on countless weekends and nightshifts. The product of his work is a clear and motivating layout, modern graphics, and brilliant photo work.

Jens Klatt for all the good times we had together shooting the pictures for this book, and his persistence in the digital processing of the material.

Ingrid Schlott for her patience in proof-reading.

Peter Musch for his insightful German correction and the English translation.

Cameron Paul for his passionate english correction.

Dieter Singer from the "Verband deutscher Kanuschulen" for his didactic revision.

The Versam Canoe School, Switzerland, for the insights into their outstanding way of teaching.

Michael Neumann of the German "KANUmagazin", Sebastian Gruendler and Manuel Arnu for additional images.

Olaf, Manuel, Jens for their constructive, wise criticism and opinions regarding the most varying topics.

My sponsors: Andy Knight from Palm / Dagger Europe, Goran Langgard from Sweet, Robert Sommer from Robson, Horst Fuersattel from hf, Herve Chabert from Patagonia and Ronald Muehlboeck from Adidas eyewear.

How to use this book

There is a lot more to becoming a superior paddler than simply refining your technical paddling skills. The environment demands sound basic knowledge and a variety of skills. The pillars of canoe schooling illustrate the different components of the training:

White water anatomy and hydrodynamics.
Technique; the development of a feeling for the boat and familiarity with the water.
Tactics and maneuvers.
Head work; additional content such as swift water rescue skills, group behavior, equipment, organization, ecology, psychology, fitness and philosophy.

Positive development is based on parallel improvement in all areas; Concentric learning.

This book offers techniques, tactics and basic knowledge for every class of white water. Thus the beginner is able to follow the book chronologically, and the advanced paddler can enter at any level, finding valuable information about

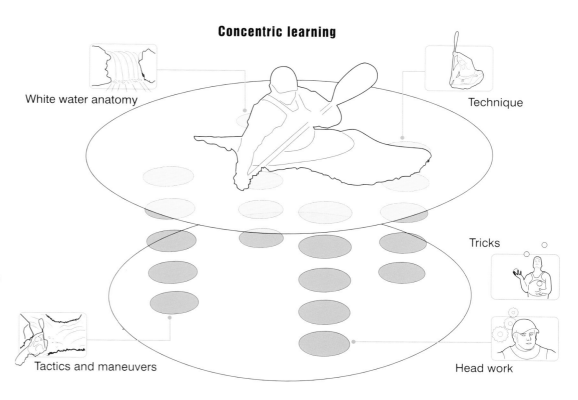

Concentric learning

White water anatomy

Technique

Tricks

Head work

Tactics and maneuvers

all aspects of white water:

(01) Flat water: Learn the basic techniques.

(02) Moving water; class 1: Learn the basic tactics and maneuvers.

(03) White water; class 2-3: Learn to judge moderately difficult white water and how to put all the basics together for a successful run.

(04) Extreme white water; class 4-5: Paddling at your personal limit in class 4-5 white water.

Checking technique on a regular basis is important not only for novices, it is also a prerequisite for advanced to expert paddlers in order to achieve continuous further development. You can check each other or use a video camera, but for most of you an approved instructing "pro" will help best.

Learning how to paddle

Where do I go, if I want to learn white water kayaking?
Every stretch of water, every lake and every river has its "boating tradition". In a myriad of different forms, people living at the banks have always had floating craft that served as a boat.

It is best to check the internet for a local canoe or kayak club, or to find a professional canoe/kayak school in your area which offers weekend or holiday classes for all skill levels. In the following I have listed some useful web addresses for your first contact with schools or clubs:

> **Tip**

> If you have sound basic knowledge you can choose to simply read the tips and only go deeper into the text if required. The gray shaded sections offer useful additional knowledge.

www.vdks.de
(German Canoe School Association)

www.kanu.de
(German Canoe Association)

www.kanuschule.ch
(Versam Kayak School)

www.gene17.com
(Simon Westgarth' Kayak School)

www.teamtarkio.com
(Montana, US based kayak school)

www.kanukurse.de
(Canyon Kayak School)

www.freeflowkayak.com
(Kayak School of Francesco Salvato)

www.olligrau.de
(Olli Grau)

www.kayakojacko.co.uk
(Kayak School of Andy Jackson)

www.kanuverband.at
(Austrian Canoe Association)

www.swisscanoe.ch
(Swiss Canoe Association)

www.bcu.org.uk
(British Canoe Union)

www.americanwhitewater.org
(American Whitewater Association)

www.canoe-europe.org
(European Association)

www.canoeicf.com
(World Association)

> **Tip**

Important additional skills for paddlers include:

> First aid, especially the treatment of shoulder dislocations and hypothermia.

> Rope handling and knot skills from rock climbing.

> Ecologically correct behavior.

Getting used to the boat, learning the basic techniques

Flat water

Every novice starts out on flat or still water. Regardless of age, sex and physical condition, it does not take long to learn the basic paddling skills on a lake. But it also makes sense for an advanced boater to train techniques on flat water over and over again.

Mirror Lake in Britisch Columbia, Canada

I always returned to my home lake to simply get wet or to practice the Eskimo roll. The quiet, warm water of a lake offers an ideal training ground. If you want to work on your paddling skills during the winter months, you might rather go to an indoor swimming pool. Many clubs and canoe schools offer indoor pool training classes.

Tuaton Lake, Northern British Columbia

Equipment

Kayaking is a sport which requires a number of pieces of equipment to work and play with, but basically one set of gear does it all – any conditions, any river.

For your first attempts on a lake you don't need all the fancy gear you will have later on. Your best option is to join a club or to take a class at a canoe school and let them take care of the gear for you. Alternatively, find a store which offers beginner classes and provides you with test material. If you want to start on your own, simply rent yourself a boat, a spray skirt and a paddle from your local dealer. Even though you will acquire sound knowledge about paddling in the following chapters, it is essential to have an expert such as your local kayak retailer around when it comes to finding gear that individually suits you and your skills. A standard set of gear for a kayak novice costs between €1,000 and €1,400.

Adjusting the boat

The seat should have direct contact to your hips to give you maximum boat control. Since most of the seats on the market are made to fit the B.B.P. (Biggest Bottom Possible), you have to scale them down with seat fittings.

These fittings made of mini-cell foam are available at your local boat retailer. Shape them with a rasp or with rough sandpaper, so that they neither squeeze you in the boat, nor make it hard to get into or out of the cockpit. Sand their back side also and then glue them to the side walls of your seat with contact adhesive. Adjust your back rest and your foot rests tightly, so that both thighs have contact with the thigh braces, even in a relaxed sitting position. If the thigh braces are adjustable, they should be positioned so that they have the greatest possible area of contact with your inner thighs.

Boat

A beginner's boat should be stable, should track well, and should have a large cockpit. Boats with a length of 2,50 – 3,00 meters are excellently suited for your first attempts on a lake or on white water.

A white water kayak normally has different features for individual adjustment. Take your time to make these first adjustments properly – the more comfortably you sit, the more fun you'll have. Furthermore, the more direct your contact is with the boat, the easier it is to control.

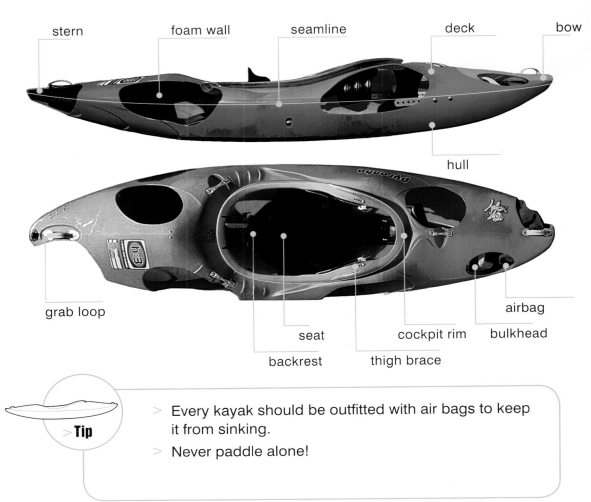

stern   foam wall   seamline   deck   bow

hull

grab loop   seat   backrest   thigh brace   cockpit rim   bulkhead   airbag

> **Tip**
> > Every kayak should be outfitted with air bags to keep it from sinking.
> > Never paddle alone!

Seat fittings

The most important fittings are the hip fittings. They are ergonomically shaped, cover the legs between hip and the base of the thigh, and allow you to edge your boat more directly.

Covering the base of your seat with a foam mat not only keeps your backside warm, but also gives it better traction. A triangular piece of foam between your thighs at the very front of your seat keeps you from sliding forward.

If the thigh braces pinch, you should modify them with pieces of foam in order to make them fit over a larger area. If your knees are pinched against the hull of the boat, it is helpful to use foam spacers on the inside of the hull.

If you are facing long portages it is very helpful to cover the inside of your gunwale, between thigh brace and seat, with small pieces of foam.

Foam spacers for the knees

Hip pads

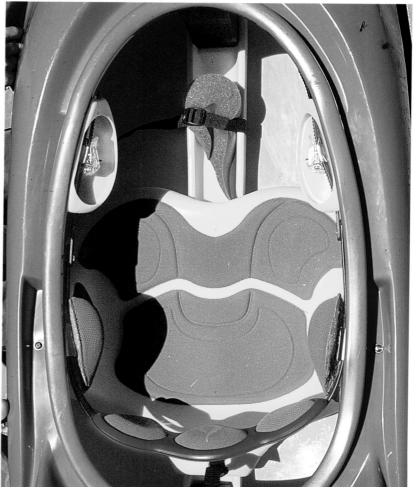

16

Paddle

Both paddle and spray skirt are a kayaker's life insurance. The loss or the damage of one of these pieces of gear can have fatal consequences in difficult white water. The characteristics of a good paddle are the same for the beginner as well as for the expert. A paddle needs a durable shaft, solid blades, and should be capable of withstanding repeated contact with rocks. If you want to paddle challenging white water you will need to spend at least €160 on a paddle with an overall weight of 800 – 1200 grams.

The shaft of the paddle is oval where you grip it, in order to let you feel the right position of the blades. An oval grip also avoids an unintended turning of the paddle on contact with rocks or other obstacles.

Paddle shafts are normally made out of aluminum or fiberglass, whereby fiberglass has the most advantages: it is warm, flexible and resilient. Carbon shafts, which are very light and stiff, are mostly used only for white water racing.

Paddle blades for beginners are ideally symmetrical and curved along their length, giving the blade a better "grip" on the water and forward propulsion. Modern blades are manufactured out of plastic materials and technologies borrowed from aircraft construction or Formula One. Pre-Preg paddles or Carbon-Kevlar laminates are expensive but extremely light and strong. Less expensive injection molded or polyethylene paddles are also solid, but are considerably heavier.

The paddle blades are rotated clockwise for ergonomic reasons. For white water use, an offset of 35°–60 ° is best. The length of the paddle is related to body height, strength, intended use and, last but not least, the length of the boat. Adults normally use a paddle length between 194cm and 202cm.

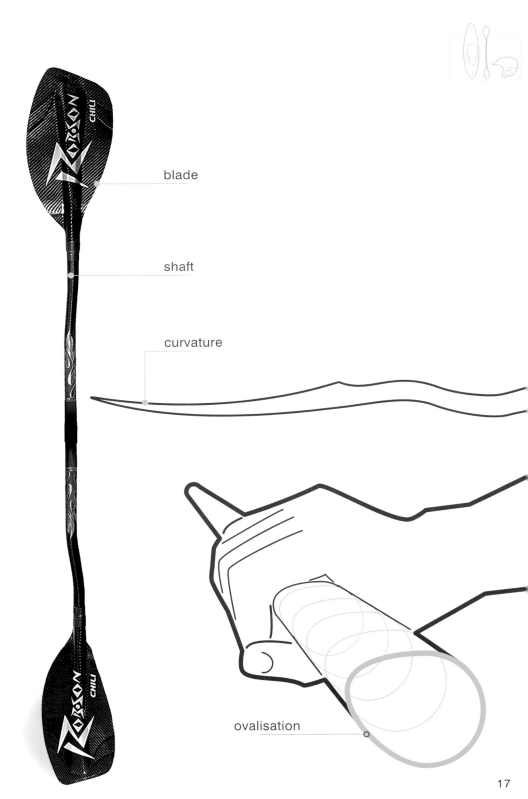

blade

shaft

curvature

ovalisation

Special paddles

Asymmetrical blades

Blades are shaped asymmetrically in order to exert pressure quickly and effectively, and to avoid rotational forces along the longitudinal axis. You can differentiate between shapes appropriate for flat strokes, as for touring or relaxed white water paddling, and shapes for steep and more vertical strokes as used in white water slalom. The flat asymmetrical shapes are best suited for most kayakers, whereas the kinetic shape for slalom use requires a technically experienced paddler.

The curvature of the blades differs also; a slalom blade, for example, is curved like a spoon in both the longitudinal and the latitudinal axis. This makes it very effective, but demands skilled paddle control. Regular white water paddles for "weekend warriors" are normally only curved along the longitudinal axis.

Manufacturers in the US also produce a so-called "Hydrowing". These paddles have a rib down the centre of the face of the blade, forming a double concave on the face, and the two halves arch forward from their center line. This leads to an improved, more controlled flow of water across both sides of the blade, and higher efficiency. Which blade you finally choose is up to both your personal preference and your technique.

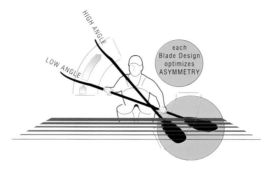

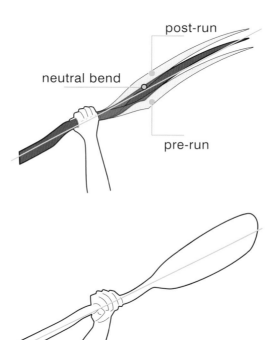

Graphics: Courtesy of WERNER Paddles.

Ergo shafts

A straight, neutral wrist position helps you to exert maximum power on your paddle blade. In order to get as close as possible to this ideal position, shafts with differing bends were developed.

It is important to differentiate between shafts which are bent in 2 and 3 dimensions.

2D bent shafts have their origin in slalom paddling and are very well suited to performing bow rudders, forward and draw strokes. In addition, the blade follows the hand a few centimeters further while doing a forward stroke (the so-called post-run), thus the paddle stabilizes and the range of action increases. The disadvantage of these paddles lies in the fact that they do not perform as well with back strokes and braces – the stabilizing effect vanishes and they tend to become unstable in your hand.

The latest developments are 2D bent shafts (so-called "neutral bent shafts") with neither pre- nor post-run. These are definitely the best choice for white water paddling.

3D bent shafts were developed for white water rodeo. These shafts usually have a pre-run so the paddle stabilizes itself during low braces and backstrokes. If you do a lot of play boating and have problems with your wrists, these paddles come well recommended.

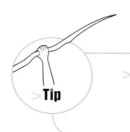

> **Tip** > For paddlers with tennis elbow or other lower arm inflammations, bent-shaft paddles can be the solution to the problem!

Spray skirts

A spray skirt covers the cockpit of a kayak and keeps the water out. It consists of a tunnel and a deck. A bungy cord forms the circumference of the deck, and this fits underneath the cockpit rim, thus connecting the spray skirt with the boat. The tunnel covers and warms your trunk and kidneys.

For a beginner the spray skirt should be easy to pull on and off. If you plan to go white water paddling later on, you are better to use a neoprene skirt right away, because they seal better than the plastic ones, and fit better to your paddling jacket. Not every spray skirt fits on every boat. To choose the right one, check with your local boat shop.

deck   tunnel

grab loop   bungee cord

Ear plugs

Ear plugs can also be a useful accessory. Cold water can cause pain in your ear canal, and can even cause undesirable bone growth in your ear, and a narrowing of the ear canal in the longer term.

Life jacket

Get used to wearing a life jacket. A kayak vest should not hinder your freedom of movement, and should have a short, waist-high cut which does not touch the spray skirt or reach above your shoulders.

Good PFD's (personal flotation devices) can be properly adjusted and should fit snugly around your upper body.

A PFD must have, according to Euro Norm, a minimum flotation of 50 kN. More than 80 kN flotation is not suited for white water paddling, since it becomes more difficult to change sides during an Eskimo roll.

A strap around your chest with a "panic lock" should be standard. Together with two shoulder straps, this forms a chest harness which can be essential for rescue or climbing efforts. After two or three years you should definitely check the flotation of your PFD, since the foam inside the vest tends to shrink after a certain time. And with it so does the buoyancy. A few manufacturers offer replacement of the worn out foam, with some vests you even have the possibility, thanks to Velcro technology, of doing this yourself.

Nose plugs

Even though a nose plug doesn't necessarily look cool, it is an effective means of keeping your sinus from a painful cold water flushing. What's more, both capsize exercises and roll training are twice as much fun without water up your nose!

...**A**rnd Schaeftlein,
Kakapotahi river, NZL

Technique

Carrying your boat

Normally you carry your boat on your shoulder. Using your paddle as a hiking pole helps you to carry it even in demanding terrain.
First you should put the boat on its stern, grab inside the cockpit rim with your hand, lift and balance the boat onto your shoulder. Another possibility is to lift the boat horizontally by the

cockpit rim, balance it on your thigh and then put it on your shoulder.
For longer distances it is preferable to carry the boat with the back rest on your fore head, stabilizing it with one hand at the stern end of the cockpit rim.
For very long distances it makes sense to tie it to a back pack or to purchase a special carrying system.

Dry training

Before you get into your boat for the first time, you should get used to the offset of the paddle blades and practice the forward stroke on land. Without these warm up exercises the paddle can easily hit the boat, mostly resulting in a capsize.

Tip

> If you are traversing a steep hill, make sure that you carry your kayak on the downhill side. If you slip, you can catch yourself with the uphill hand, or simply sit down.

Grip width

Hold your paddle with both hands and place it on your head. To get the optimum width for your grip, the angle between your fore- and upper arm should be a little less than 90°. The oval grip of the shaft lies comfortably between the second and the third finger joint. The grip is the same as for carrying a heavy suitcase.

Holding and turning the paddle

Next, get into your boat on the land and simulate the forward stroke with a proper turn of the paddle. You should sit with a straight back and a slight forward lean. Stretch out both arms while holding your right hand in front of your chest and the left one in front of your forehead. Dig your paddle blade into the "water" next to your feet, making sure that the inner curve of your paddle is facing towards the back of the boat. In order to obtain a better forward reach, you should rotate your upper body;

Optimum grip width

passive side passive side

active side active side

a Dig in the paddle next to your feet

b Rotate upperbody

c Turn the paddle with your right hand

d Tighten your grip for the next stroke

bring the right shoulder forward and the left one back.

This is the only way to get a powerful stroke, because the main power for a forward stroke comes from proper torso rotation, and not only from your arms.

Now lead your paddle blade along the boat,

Paddle bridge

Underwater exit

Push off the bank

bring your left shoulder forward and the right one back. During the last phase, bend your right arm to a maximum of 90°, until your elbow is next to your torso.

Now change the paddle side: Bring the left blade forward, next to your feet. Before you dig the blade in again, you have to turn the concave face of the paddle to face backwards by turning the right hand end of the shaft like the throttle of a motorcycle.

You must practice this series of motions repeatedly until the movement becomes automatic.

Entering and exiting your kayak

It is essential to practice both entering and exiting your boat before you get into the water for the first time.

Once you are in the water, you first have to practice capsizing and exiting. It makes it a lot easier to learn paddling, if you know you are able to get out of your boat quickly and effortlessly.

Here's a few tips for the underwater exit:
First practice without, and then with your spray skirt on.

Always open the spray skirt with your hands (not your knees).

Open your eyes under water and either blow a little air out of your nose or use a nose plug. With both hands on the edge of the cockpit, slide your hips out of the boat, keeping your upper body leaning forward.

Return your head to the surface of the water only once your legs are completely out of the boat.

> **Tip**

> First practice without and then with your spray skirt on.
> Always open the spray skirt with your hands.
> Open your eyes under water and either blow a little air out of your nose or use a nose plug right away.
> Push your hips out of the boat with both hands and keep your upper body in forward lean position.
> Only return your head to the surface of the water, once your legs are completely out of the boat.

The seating position

Sitting properly and the trim of the boat

A basic prerequisite is mobility in the lumbar part of your upper body. This enables you to react to turbulence, to tilt the boat, and to rotate your whole upper body. The lower vertebrae are the main pivot point for a paddler, connecting the static base (the boat) with the dynamically active upper body. This agility can only be reached through proper body position. Consequently it is important to practice it right from the start, even though this seems to take a lot of effort. It is far more comfortable to lean against your backrest with a slightly bent back, but this will prevent you from getting any effective transfer of power.

Sit upright in your boat with your upper body bent slightly forward. Try to get away from the backrest, keeping your weight on your buttocks. Your legs are spread and held against the thigh braces. Your ankles are kept together on the bottom of the boat and balls of your feet are pushed against the foot rest. In this position your dorsal vertebra is held in a neutral position, allowing "active lateral tilting" and a preventive bending to absorb shocks.

This basic position is also a prerequisite for the "positive tension" of your whole body. Your stomach muscles are tensed and help you to transmit your power directly from your paddle to the boat.

Another advantage of this position is the neutral position of your body to both the bow and the stern, which makes it a lot easier to find an optimal trim for the boat. Only with the right trim does the boat have neutral paddling performance. This particular adjustment is made by sliding the seat forward or backward. Roughly speaking it should be adjusted so that the bow is 2.5 cm higher above the water surface than the stern.

Correct seating position: upper body leaning slightly forward

Paddling forward

Once you are in the water, you will quickly find that it takes sensitive paddling to keep the boat on a straight course. You need to adjust your direction anew with every stroke. A stronger stroke on the right side and the boat turns left – and vice versa! The more precisely you carry out your stroke along the edge of the boat, the straighter your forward momentum becomes. After a while you will have automated your forward strokes and will know how to keep the boat going in a straight line.

But beware – proper forward paddling involves more than keeping your boat on a straight trajectory! An ergonomic forward stroke is the result of innumerable river kilometres.

Don't forget to check your seating position over and over again – dig the whole paddle blade in as far forward as possible and rotate your upper body along with the stroke.

> Tip

> Be aware of your torso rotation! Bring the active shoulder forward and hold your paddle as relaxed and easily as possible! If your active wrist joint is not completely straight in this position, check your grip of the paddle shaft, and whether you have twisted your upper body all the way to the side!

a Dig the paddle in as far forward as possible

b Make the stroke close to the boat

c Change sides

d Rotate your upper body

The paddle box

Since it is fairly difficult to get up speed in modern white water boats, it really does make sense to optimize your paddle strokes, the most important being the forward stroke. The rotation of the upper body in this case is your turbo charger for an effective stroke, because the power comes from a properly rotated upper body, and not from your biceps. Take this as one of the most important principles of the modern paddling technique. Your arms are an extension to your torso, and only work as levers. The wrist joints, the elbows and the shoulders are only good for the fine tuning. In order to use the comparatively weak arm joints properly, you need to form the so-called paddle box with your arms and the paddle. In this way you obtain the best compromise between lever forces and muscle potential. Your lower arm and the back of your hand should be aligned, your lower and your upper arm should be at an angle of 110° to 120°, whereas the upper arm and your collarbone should be at an angle of 150° – seen from above. With the help of small adjustments you should always try to maintain this paddle box.

The paddle box is the basic position for your arms

Flat forward stroke/ Cruising

The way that I explained the forward stroke gives you maximum forward speed. But often, if you just want to hang out and drift along with the current, there is no need for such a powerful stroke – you just need a little speed to control the boat. This can be achieved mainly with your arms – no need for torso rotation. This means the upper hand does not reach any higher than your chest. Now relax and enjoy!

Sweep stroke

The sweep stroke is carried out with a straight arm acting around your torso. On the water it draws an arc around the paddler, and is good for initiating a turn or to straighten up a boat that has run off course.

For the set up of the sweep stroke you must rotate your upper body and bring your active shoulder forward. Dig your paddle in next to your feet, but keep the shaft lower than you would for a forward stroke, keeping the opposite hand chest high or even lower.

Now draw the paddle away from the boat in a large arc and around your body. During the stroke the active arm remains as straight as possible, whereas the opposite arm is kept bent and chest high.

Stern rudder

As long as the boat still has a certain forward momentum, you can achieve an additional turning impulse by keeping the blade at the back of the boat at the end of the sweep stroke and turning the face of the paddle towards your body. It will now work as a rudder and amplify the turning impulse. This phase of the sweep stroke is called stern rudder.

> **Tip**

> Both for the sweep and the forward stroke, your weight always remains equally distributed on your buttocks to keep your boat flat and your center of gravity directly above it.

Directing your gaze

Your head guides your body. If you look over your shoulder you automatically rotate your upper body in the same direction. This statement is as true as it is simple. In practice, for any paddling novice this means that if you fail to go straight while paddling forward, you should keep looking in the direction you want to go, and your upper body will already be perfectly positioned for a corrective stroke. If you want to turn the boat, look in the desired direction as early as possible. Your gaze will become tactically more important later on in white water. You will start to focus on so-called anchor points in order to maneuver your boat, for example, through a cataract. Fixing your gaze on the point that you are heading for will always bring your upper body into the correct position for the correct strokes.

a Rotate your upper body in the new direction of travel

b Push the paddle away from the boat in a big arc…

c …until it is close to your body again

Edging and bracing

Edging your boat, with or without leaning your body, and bracing, are basic moves for flowing water. Once you are able to handle these techniques properly, you will hardly capsize anymore, plus you will have the best ingredients for the Eskimo roll. Just like so many other things, it makes sense to first practice these edging and bracing techniques on dry land and without a boat.

Learning to edge

Basically, edging works according to the following principle: you transfer your weight onto **one** of your buttocks and, to avoid capsizing, **you** bend your torso sideways, keeping your **point** of gravity directly above the boat.

Sit down on the floor in a kayaking position, **holding** your paddle – fairly upright with a slight **forward** lean. Now grab your paddle and **keep your** elbows right above your straightened **wrist** joints. Now shift your weight to one **of your** buttocks and counterbalance this position by **bringing** your head and your torso to **the opposite** side. Practice this balance movement **without your** paddle touching the ground **and make sure** that you use your hip, torso **and head together** to carry out this stabilizing **move.**

Paddle brace

As soon as your center of gravity moves away from the boat's longitudinal center line, you are in danger of capsizing. One way to avoid this capsize is the paddle brace.

Still on the bank and from this simulated seating position, let yourself fall sideways while bending your upper body in the other direction, as you would do to edge the boat. Avoid landing in the dirt by leaning on the back of your onside paddle blade.

The paddle brace brings you back into the neutral position; push yourself away hard from the paddle and flick your hip back in one go, to get back onto both buttocks. This sideways bend goes all the way along your spine to your head. As a consequence your head returns to the upright position above the boat.

This move is called "C to C" because of the fast bending of the vertebra from one side to the other. This is a basis for edging, bracing and the Eskimo roll.

Bracing is a lot more difficult in the water, since your paddle sinks if you simply lean on it. Here bracing, bending and flicking of the hip, and pushing off the paddle blade have to be carried out explosively and simultaneously. Practice this move in the beginning by supporting yourself on the bank, and learn to coordinate the three parts of this move before you start in deeper water.

> Tip

> Keep your head deliberately over the longitudinal center line of the boat when you are edging the boat, and shift it to the active side as soon as you bring your boat back into the neutral position.

> Try to do a small forward arc with your active blade while you are bracing – in doing so you keep your paddle on the surface a little longer.

a Starting position | **b** edge and brace... | **c** ...back

Edging and bracing - as action or reaction!

Edging and bracing are not only reactions to an imminent capsize, but are vital elements to many maneuvers in flowing water. For example, if you are eddying out you should lean into the turn as you would do on a bike. You tilt the boat and lean yourself actively into the inside of the turn. With this outrigging movement you work against the momentum of fast currents, and the paddle brace brings you back into the neutral position.

Edging with an outrigging move while eddying out

> Tip

> In turbulent situations braces are also used provisionally, without tilting and outrigging, to stabilize the boat.

■ sequenz **a** Neutral position with the elbows pointing up

■ sequenz **b** Bracing dynamically

■ sequenz **c** Bring your head back over the boat last

Warming sunshine in a deep gorge,
Stikine River, Canada

Tactics and maneuvers

Automation of the techniques

As soon as you can handle the forward and the sweep stroke you need to "automate" these techniques, meaning that you carry them out without even thinking about them. And this means practice, a lot of practice.

Do a zigzag course on a lake and try to approach trees or other targets in the straightest line possible. Play ball games on the water with your friends and practice canoe polo by throwing into goals.

Goals

In order to keep yourself motivated, it is essential to set goals. One for the next ten minutes, one for the day and one for the whole week. Such a learning goal can be a good straight line in your boat, a technical course around a little island or anything else that requires you to handle your boat. Practice until your boat does exactly what you want it to.

Head work

Stay yourself

Seen from an outside point of view, kayaking is an individual sport that is carried out in groups. In the unfamiliar element of water, fear will always play a role. You will learn to listen to your inner voice and to interpret your moods and emotions. Just because one of your training partners is quickly getting used to a new situation does not necessarily mean the same is true for you. Be honest with yourself, only then can you recognize your next goal and master it.

Getting used to water

Even though a small, clean, warm lake does not scare anyone who can swim, the fear factor that I mentioned above comes into play as soon as a novice has to sit in a kayak for the first time. Whoa! You squeeze yourself into some kind of plastic barrel that seems anything but stable, and all you get to keep yourself upright is a stupid paddle which you can barely manage on land? No way!

So you need to lose the fear, and the first step is learning to get out of your boat nice and easily. Only without fear will you experience real learning progress. So, if you are having problems exiting the kayak underwater because you lose your orientation, try the same thing again on the beach. After this, go back into chest deep water, without the boat, turn upside down and keep your eyes open. Only once you are able to keep your orientation should you get back into the boat and capsize.

Getting used to water is one of the most essential steps to take before you come in contact with white water. Even today I still wet my face and my neck with a handful of water as soon as I enter my boat, just so as not to let the first wave startle me. Honestly!

In New Zealand the very structure of the car is put to the test

Tricks

Loading boats

If you want to transport a kayak properly you have to use a roof rack and straps or ropes. Sounds pretty simple, huh? But have you ever tried losing three boats in the five o'clock rush hour, doing 140 kilometres an hour? Ok, so let's talk about getting these missiles fixed, and I mean bombproof!

The ideal solution is if you can screw your roof rack into a rail which is pre-mounted on the car's roof. Gutters have more or less disappeared for aerodynamic reasons, and only classic cars like the Land Rover still have them.

The distance between the spars should normally exceed the length of the cockpit; the best length is 95cm. This allows you to fix the boats without tying their ends down. The best thing for fixing your boat on the rack are straps with metal locks. If you are using ropes, make sure you know some knots that hold, but can be undone easily. If you normally only carry one or two boats you will not need anything like a vertical or oval metal post. Firstly, they make a lot of noise and, secondly, they are easily lost on the doorway of a car port!

If you are loading one or two boats, put them on the rack with the stern facing forwards and the cockpit facing down. Bonus points are scored if the cockpit rim hooks into one of the spars! Use at least one strap per spar, and make sure that the strap goes around the spar between the boats! (This was my mistake as the boats flew off the roof at 140km/h on the motorway!) Take care to keep the strap between boat and spar vertical. This makes for the shortest route and it keeps the boat from slipping sideways. Tighten the strap firmly, but ensure that the shell of the kayak does not get deformed or dented by the pressure.

If you have to load four or more boats, it's time for the vertical post. The boats are placed stern to bow, whereby two boats are always tied together cockpit to cockpit on the vertical post. If you don't have such a vertical post, go for the "double 69". Here a boat is placed on the roof rack, cockpit up, and another on top, cockpit down, facing in the other direction. The picture will show you what I am talking about. Make sure that the boats are of similar length, and that both straps (one per spar!) are positioned near the ends of the kayaks. Otherwise a kayak can be squeezed out.

Cockpit covers are good for saving gas and for loading extra gear.

Aerodynamic position for one kayak

Two kayaks in a 69

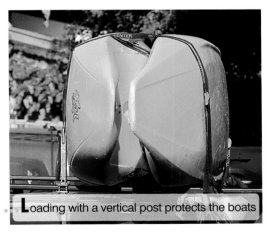

Loading with a vertical post protects the boats

> **Tip**

> If your straps start "singing" at certain speeds, simply twist the parts of the strap which are not in contact with the boat.

Eskimo roll

For the Eskimo people in the Arctic sea, the Eskimo roll is a technique of pure survival in the freezing cold water. For us white water warriors, the roll is almost as important. Once you are able to handle your boat well in flat water and the paddle no longer feels totally alien to you, it is time to learn the "roll". As you start to make the first maneuvers in moving water, being able to roll takes away the fear of a mistake which can lead to capsizing – and if you should happen to capsize, you don't lose precious learning time with swimming, dumping and recovering your kayak.

The best way to learn the roll is with a friend or an experienced coach, giving you advice and tips in every learning phase. A warm pool or a nice lake in the summer are both well suited to quick and efficient learning. Allow yourself a few afternoons' time to learn the roll, take it easy, and allow your body time to get used to this completely new situation and movement.

Orientation upside down

Before you start with your roll training you need to get used to being upside down in your boat. This means that you remain seated, don't panic, and still know where the left or the right side is. If you are having problems, grab yourself a diving mask and practice exiting your boat slowly; nice and easy!

"Flick yer hipz"

The next step is to transfer the bend and flick of your hips, torso and head, which you are now familiar with from bracing, to a complete capsize situation. To begin, hold onto the edge of the pool or the helping hands of your trainer with both hands next to your head, and capsize the boat. In the beginning, keep your head above the water and set your boat upright with a flick of the hips. Pull your lower knee towards your chest while you leave your head on the surface and look at your bow. Again you use the "C to C" position that you already know from bracing. And now – practice, practice, practice!

Beware! Your spine plays a major role in this movement, and can only be effective if it remains in a neutral position – you must avoid leaning back. If your bow stays closer to the edge of the pool than your stern in a slight forward lean, then you have the right seat position.

The further you capsize your boat, the more you have to twist your upper body sideways to reach the surface with both hands. Along with bending the upper body sideways comes a torso rotation. If you are capsized to the right (as in the illustration below), your torso is both bent and rotated to the left.

> Tip

> It is helpful to practice the roll with a nose plug or a diving mask.
> Get your partner to hold your head so you can get a feel for bending from your knee to your hip through your torso and all the way to your head.

As you get back up, your torso tilts and rotates from left to right.

Once you are in a complete capsize position, you must follow your hands with your eyes while righting yourself. Keep looking at your hands until you are completely vertical again. By watching your hands you lead with your head, and thus encourage the correct bending and rotation of the torso and hips throughout the movement. Pull the boat underneath your body with the lower knee and push yourself onto the surface with your hands. Do not bring your upper body into an upright seating position until the boat is completely upright, the hull sitting flat on the water.

Once you can perform the hip bend and flick you hardly need any extra power to get your boat back up. When you can carry the whole movement out with only two fingers on the edge of the pool, it's time to grab the paddle!

sequenz **a b**   Warm up exercise for the roll; the trainer holds your head just above the surface

Sweep stroke roll – the whitewater roll

Of the numerous different rolling techniques, the sweep stroke roll is for me the one which offers the most advantages. By bending and rotating your upper body you are able to make full use of your torso muscles, while keeping your "weak" arms and your "endangered" shoulders in a stable, almost static position.

The more you get used to the paddle, the easier rolling becomes, and having somebody to hold and guide your paddle now will be of great help. If you have to work and train on your own, it is helpful if you duct-tape a foam board to your paddle blade in order to improve its flotation.

> Tip

> Hold your paddle as relaxed as possible! If the active wrist joint is not completely straight in this position, check your grip of the paddle and whether you have rotated your upper body all the way to the side.

with your lower arms. Look to your front (right) hand and check the position of your blades. The face of the front blade must be flat on the surface of the water (facing downwards towards you), whereby the back elbow touches the torso and the front one is slightly bent.

Starting position

Most people first learn to roll on their right side. For the starting position, bend and twist your torso sideways to the left with your right hand forward, and hold the paddle parallel to the left side of the boat. Tilt your left hip up to meet the body. This 'scrunched up' position is like a coiled spring, ready to be released and flick the boat back upright.
Now capsize and push the paddle completely back to the surface, so that you touch the boat

Rolling up

Keep the front blade on the surface and sweep it in a wide arc away from the boat, while keeping your left elbow tightly against the body. As soon as you start this paddle movement, pull your right knee underneath your body and flick your hip back to the left. Keep looking at your right hand, to make sure your upper body rotates to the right along with the paddle, and then pull yourself over the paddle with your arms.

a Start rolling up with your eye on your active hand which is at the surface

b Pull your left knee towards your chest (roll on the left side)

c Looking constantly at your hands while rolling

Final position

At the end of the roll movement, your upper body is in a forward leaning position, twisted towards the stroking (in this case right) side above the boat. Your arms are in the starting position for the high brace (see p. 89) with the elbows facing down. The left arm is strongly bent and the left hand is right in front of the left shoulder. Your head is facing the active hand on the right blade, which remains in the water, behind your body. In order to build up tension, pull both knees towards your body.

This final position results from the correct movement of the paddle across the water surface and a slightly bent back arm, the correct bend and flick of hip and torso, and torso rotation. From this position you can quickly carry out a brace if required, or continue with a strong paddle stroke.

It makes a lot of sense to practice and learn the roll on both sides, right from the beginning. Nonetheless, you will always have a "chocolate side".

> Tip

> Flicking your hip and sweeping the paddle must be synchronized!

In white water

If you are transferring your rolling technique to white water, it makes a lot of sense to start in a slight current and gradually work your way up to stronger ones.

In white water you normally roll on the downstream side. Should this not be possible – if the river is not deep enough to roll through – you have to try the slightly more difficult upstream roll, in which the paddle often gets pushed down by the current.
Generally speaking you should favor "rolling through". Sometimes you even succeed in bringing your paddle into a proper rolling position just the second before you capsize. This means taking some momentum along with you and rolling with a good "schwiing". Bracing until the very end gets you into a bad position and is punished with the time you need aligning your paddle underwater.

a Starting position, looking at your active hand

b Paddle remains on the surface

c Synchronize the hip flick with the stroke of the paddle

d Final position, looking towards the active hand

Farewell high brace roll

There are numerous different rolling techniques, but the one described above seems to me to be the best suited for beginners and advanced paddlers, no matter how good their physical condition is. The higher your skill level gets, the more different rolling variations you'll have. You will develop a good sense for the currents around you and how to use them to roll up again with very little effort.

One of these techniques is the so-called high brace roll. Basically you have to hold the paddle at a right angle to the boat, whereby the passive hand rests on the bottom of the hull. Now the active hand pushes the paddle to the surface. The resistance that you require for the C to C is obtained by pulling on the paddle as if doing a high brace. Practically speaking, the high brace roll is merely an extreme high brace. The technique is often taught since it brings instant learning success in flat water.

However, this roll definitely has some serious disadvantages. First of all, it is difficult to get into a proper starting position in a modern kayak, which is very wide and box shaped. It is difficult to get your paddle into a starting position parallel to the surface, since your back hand is high out of the water as a result of the shape of the hull. As a consequence you are forced to over-extend your shoulder, resulting in a very vulnerable position.

Furthermore, this roll is only suited for real white water if you have the necessary sensitivity for currents. Currents can work against the flotation of your paddle blade – the blade can get pulled down and you end up with a vertical paddle in a semi-rolled position. This is not only unfavorable for starting another attempt, but even if you have succeeded in rolling completely, you are still in an unstable position for paddling on. The main aim of the Eskimo roll should be to get safely back onto the surface, and quickly back into combat position.

The high brace roll is difficult in boats with a modern flat bottom shape

Improving your technique and your first maneuvers

Moving water; class 1

A river starts gaining speed and turns into white water. The experience begins right at that moment when the current starts carrying you along for the first time. The course of the river will surprise you over and over again. There are waves, rocks and currents you have to master, you have to both act and react constantly.
And enjoy.

The Verzasca in the Ticino region in Italy is one of the most beautiful rivers in the Alps

This chapter deals with the second group of the basic paddling techniques, whereby I do want to concentrate on the most important area; eddy-line maneuvers in the current. It is clear that everybody wants to get into the white water as soon as possible and not waste time on a lousy lake – paddling forward, edging and all the other nonsense right? But beware! White water will punish a lack of good basic skills right away! Make sure all your flat water techniques are bombproof before you take the next step forward and beyond. In your first weeks of paddling you will mainly be doing fundamental work concerning your technique. Go for a rock solid base!

White water classes of difficulty (ICF)

	Class 1	Class 2	Class 3	Class 4	Class 5	Class 6
	Easy	Moderately difficult	Difficult	Very difficult	Extremely difficult	At the limit of navigability
Line of sight		open passages	clearly visible passages	passages normally require scouting	scouting absolutely necessary	
Water	regular current regular waves and small wave trains	irregular current irregular waves mid-sized wave trains small holes, whirlpools, boils and pillows	high, irregular waves longer wave trains holes, whirlpools boils and pillows	higher, longer wave trains strong holes, whirlpools, boils and pillows	extreme wave trains extreme holes, whirlpools, boils and pillows	basically impossible, possible only at certain water levels, even then highly dangerous!
Riverbed	simple obstacles	few obstacles in the main current small ledges and drops	isolated boulders, ledges and drops other obstacles in the main current	offset blocks in the main current higher ledges and drops with recirculating holes	tightly offset boulders high ledges and drops with difficult approach or exit	

Easy technical section on the Verzasca river, Switzerland

White water anatomy

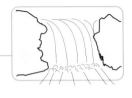

River guidebooks

A kayak run starts with the selection of a suitable section on a certain river. Since it is a fairly difficult job to find the right one for you and your group, either follow locals or check the information contained in guidebooks.

Difficulty

The difficulty of a certain river section is always the main criteria for selection. As a novice coming from a nearby lake, you will probably go for some class 1 or 2 rapids. If you are used to moving water, familiar with eddy techniques and the roll, you should definitely check out some of the class 2 or 3 runs. But it is obligatory in any case to have some paddling friends and partners with you on the river – buddies you can rely on, and who can help you in case things turn tricky.

The difficulty of a certain run is always determined by the main part or key section of that particular stretch. Exceptionally difficult or unboatable passages are referred to in brackets, for example 2(4). 2+ stands for a difficult class 2 with few eddies, for example, whereas 2- is easier.

The discussion about river difficulties and their rating is never ending, and new systems and standards are being developed constantly. However, any classification, no matter how simple or complicated it may be, is always subjective. It depends largely on the personal interpretation of the particular author. As a consequence, the classification in a river guide book can only serve as a rough orientation, and it is vital to check the actual situation and the water level yourself, before you put in!

Gradient

Water starts to move as soon as the riverbed has a gradient, which is measured in thousandths. 3 thousandths stand for 3 meters of gradient per 1 kilometre of river length. Even though this sounds quite small, this could refer to the powerful class 3 Imster Schlucht of the Inn River in Austria. Steep, yet boatable rivers, have up to 120 thousandths of gradient.

Volume

The water volume has a decisive influence on the character of a white water river. In Europe it is measured in cubic meters per second. A big river like the Rhine has an average of 1600 cubic meters per second. The Isar in Munich averages at about 65 cubic meters per second. Every river has different periods in which it has different water levels. High water can be caused by strong rainfalls or by snowmelt in spring. Low water levels are normally caused by dry, cold weather. In the Alps we differentiate between glacial rivers (Oetztaler Ache, Dora Baltea) and rivers that are fed by snow melt (Sanna, Saalach). A lot of rivers get

Flood

High flow

Medium flow

Low flow

...The riverbed can indicate certain water-levels, Saalach, Austria

their water from a combination of these water sources, and both the height and the relief of the catchment area play a major role in this case. For most white water runs there is an ideal water level, and this particular level is normally indicated in a river guidebook. Often there are gauges which help you to check the navigability of a certain river or section. All classifications regarding the difficulties of a river should be related to a certain water level or gauge reading in order to make the most objective judgment possible.

> Tip

> You can check many of the gauges in real-time via the internet, for example under www.kajak.at or www.kanumagazin.de for the Alps.

Bank and riverbed

A river is characterized by the type of valley it runs through; the type and geological age of the rock from which it is formed, and the relief. We differentiate between the following different types of valley: U-shaped valley, V-shaped valley and box canyon.

Rivers that are suited to novices can mostly be found in U-shaped valleys, where the river meanders through wide open terrain. Steeper and wilder rivers can be found in V-shaped valleys and box canyons, in which the water mainly follows the fall line and meanders very little. There is another factor that comes into the calculation when talking about influences on rivers and their flows: Man. The Alps are one of the most populated mountain regions on earth and this lack of space forces rivers to be channelled into ditches, or rather graves. There are only very few rivers which are still untouched and have not been straightened or fortified. Just imagine a river flowing naturally its whole way to the sea – a paddler's dream.

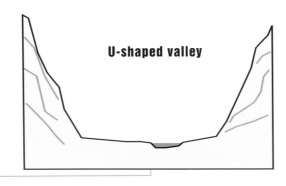

U-shaped valley

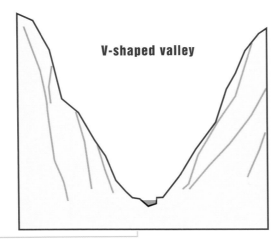

V-shaped valley

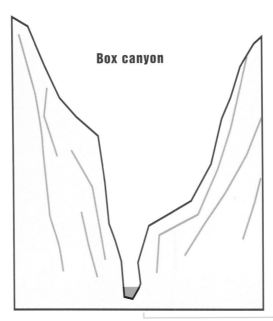

Box canyon

Avalanches can pose a danger well into the summer

Particular dangers

An obstacle that suddenly appears in front of you in a strong current is a clear hazard. Low bridges, weirs and floodgates are quite common, even on easy white water. Normally they are mentioned in river guide books, as are natural dangers such as extremely difficult or dangerous rapids.

Keep your eyes open!

Always be aware of natural risks. Even a nice easy class 2 river section can become a roaring white water nightmare overnight due to heavy rain and thunderstorms. Use your eyes and your senses and analyze your environment carefully – it's the only way to minimize risks and to stay alive on a river.

Weirs

One third of all fatal white water accidents occur in weirs on river sections that are by no means difficult or dangerous. It is very difficult for a beginner to assess the danger of a weir, along with the fact that he lacks rescue practice, and often does not carry the required safety equipment in his boat. So, if there are weirs on the river section that you are going to run, make sure to check early enough for places to stop and to get out of the boat.

Weirs are not white water! Running a weir entails dangers that not even an experienced paddler is able to assess properly at any time. Hidden pieces of metal or rotten wood barriers are only two reasons to abstain from running a weir. The most dangerous part of such a weir is the so-called back tow current, right behind the weir. This can recirculate both boat and paddler. It is essential to ascertain the length as well as the power of this current before you even think about running the weir. If you are not sure – get out of the boat and portage it. Seriously! (more about weirs: see p. 77)

Tree hazards can occur almost anywhere

The nightmare Brunauer Weir on the Oetztaler Ache

> **Tip**

> The golden rule for all weirs – if in doubt, portage!

Currents

There are many different currents in moving water, which you should consider as individual expanses or surfaces in the beginning. Seen from above, all these currents flow in different directions, and they are named as follows:

Main current

The main current follows the course of the river, is the strongest, and carries the largest amount of water. When running a river, you usually aim to be in it and thus follow the river's course.

Eddy / Eddylines

An eddy is always the starting and the finishing point of a river run, since it offers almost the only possibility of stopping on a white water river. Eddies form after narrow passages in the current, behind rocks and bridge pylons, but also at the inside of bends. The eddy is always separated from the main current by the eddy line, which is the meeting zone of two currents. Physically, an eddy results from the water's urge to even out differences in level. If the current shoots by an obstacle, water cannot fill up the "empty space" behind it from the side, and so returns back up from further down the river.

Pillows

Tight bends in a fast flowing river form so-called pillows or buffer waves. The water shoots into the outside of the turn, collides with the bank and then follows the course of the river again. These water buffers are very turbulent and quite tricky to handle for beginners. Avoid coming in contact with them by keeping your boat pointed towards the inside of the bend early enough.
Such buffers can also be found directly in front of obstacles in the middle of the current, such as rocks or bridge pylons. Stay away! (see also pages 78+89)

Main current and eddy on the Soca river, Slovenia

Pillow at the old border station in Finstermuenz, Switzerland

White water paddling requires special equipment. Always wear a life jacket and a helmet, use a spray skirt in moving water, and don't forget the throw bag. It is up to you whether or not you want to wear thermal protection wear such as a neoprene suit.

Thermal protection and paddling clothing

There is a basic rule for water temperatures below 10°C: Without thermal protection, the water temperature is equivalent to the time in minutes in which your body still has mobility, before hypothermia sets in. Normally a snowmelt fed river in May averages a water temperature of about 8° C, this means eight minutes! This is frighteningly short when you consider the time needed in the case of capsizing or rescuing a stuck boat.

Your local kayak dealer will have many different paddling jackets, neo-suits and shoes in stock to protect you from the cold.
In most cases a neoprene Long John, a tight fitting fleece sweater and a paddling jacket with waterproof seals around your neck, torso and wrists, do the best job.

Perfect outfit for moderate white water

Neoprene suit

The Long John is a sleeveless overall made out of a 0.5mm - 4 mm thick neoprene fabric, with kayak-specific features: not thicker than 4mm in order to keep your freedom of movement, not made of dive suit fabric, but of super resistant neoprene material, a pre-shaped cut that suits the seated position in a kayak, with a two-way zipper for "human needs". Depending on price, quality and intended use, manufacturers offer models with a one or two sided Polyamide, Polyester or Polypropylene laminated liner. A liner on the inside helps getting into the suit, the outside laminate makes the neo more durable.

The advantages of a neo-suit are, next to the improved thermal protection, more flotation and some extra padding in case of contact with rocks. This combination of Long John and dry jacket is still the most common and proven attire for white water paddlers.

Paddling jacket

A good paddling jacket is made out of a resistant Polyamide or Polyester fabric with a "breathable" Polyurethane (PU) coating and taped seams. This makes the jacket waterproof, but permeable for vapor, just like a good mountaineering or ski anorak. If you want to spend some extra money and go for some "real fancy stuff", get a Gore-Tex jacket, which is far more permeable for vapor than any other fabric.

The seals around wrists and neck are either simple rubber bands, giving you protection against spray water only, or waterproof latex cuffs. The hip seal also comes in different options, whereby the most common and useful one is the double waist tube. It keeps almost any spray water out, by fitting the spray skirt in between two layers of fabric around the hip. This makes the jacket, along with the latex cuffs, a "dry jacket".

Underwear

Most suited for paddling is quick-drying, functional mountain sports underwear, made of specially treated Polyester material. It offers a so-called capillary effect that draws moisture away from the skin and is still nice and cozy to wear, even if wet. Thicker materials such as Malden Mills Polartec Powerstretch or Patagonia Expeditionweight Stretch Capilene or R1 offer an exceptionally good capillary effect. These materials are great for colder water temperatures, though they dry a bit slower than traditional fleece, which offers no capillary effect.

Dry pants and dry suits

A full dry suit, or dry pants in combination with a dry jacket, are worn with suitable underwear. The advantage of these combinations is unlimited freedom of movement and unbeatable comfort.

> Tip

> Choose your outfit according to the water and not the air temperature. Most of the European white water rivers are fed by glaciers and snow melt and are damn cold!

> Using a good jacket, a waterproof boat and a fitting neoprene spray skirt keeps you dry, even in the most turbulent white water! Such a combination prolongs the season by at least a few weeks!

> When wearing a dry pant or even a dry suit, it is necessary to "deflate" the suit by releasing inside air. To do this, cower down and let the air out through one of the wrist cuffs. Having a "deflated" dry suit can be very helpful should you have to swim!

Shoes

After years of compromising, specialized paddling shoes that meet the paddler's needs have finally hit the market.

The rubber of the sole should be soft enough to offer good grip on wet and slippery rocks. The sole, with a rough tread, should be thick enough to give protection against sharp rocks, but nevertheless provide flexibility for good grip.

In any case, it is important to check how you fit in your boat with your shoes – right there in the store. They must not hinder an emergency exit!

Warm, thick neoprene shoes tend to dry very slowly and soon start to give off unpleasant odors. The best solution is thinner, quick-drying shoes that you can combine with neoprene socks if required.

Care of paddle clothing and gear

If you treat your paddle wear according to a few guidelines you will enjoy it much longer:

– Never dry your clothing, especially the latex cuffs, in direct sunlight.

– Both neoprene and outer wear should be rinsed with clean water after use.

– Never store wet clothing in closed boxes or bags, or in cars.

– You can wash and tumble dry fleece clothing in regular washing / drying machines.

– Check your gear regularly and make sure you fix small defects right away.

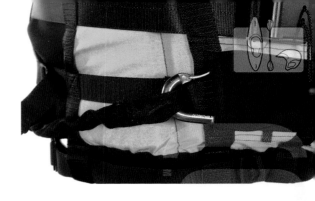

Helmets

A kayak helmet should cover and protect your forehead, your temples and the back of your head. It should fit tightly enough that you can't shake it off your head with an unlocked chin strap, should be lightweight, and should not obstruct your field of vision.

A lot of good helmets are not adjustable, but come in many different sizes and have their origin in skate and ski sports. Make sure that their lining does not absorb too much water and then become heavy. If you damage your helmet seriously, replace it!

Cowtails

Especially on fast rivers it is recommendable to carry a cowtail on your life vest. It is fixed to the rescue strap of your life vest and consists of a 1.5 meter tubular strap and a carabiner. The purpose of a cowtail is essentially to rescue an unconscious person, but it can also be used for a number of other very practical purposes, such as pulling a runaway boat out of the current.

The tubular strap should be a little longer than the stern of your boat, so that whatever you are pulling behind you can move freely from side to side.

It is essential to stow your cowtail conscientiously, and a few manufacturers offer special bags or tie the strap together with a rubber band. A loose strap can easily get caught and lead to an accident.

A cowtail should only be fixed to your life jacket with a closed metal ring, or with a locked HMS carabiner. A standard carabiner mustn't be used as it can hook itself into the life jacket, making an emergency release impossible!

Throw bag

A throw bag with 15-20 meters of floating rope and two carabiners is an essential rescue device in white water.
Holding the loose end in one hand, throw the bag towards somebody swimming in the current and then haul him back to the bank. The proper handling of the throw bag will be described in more detail in the chapter about white water safety. The throw bag must be handled with care, and the rope must be checked and dried regularly. A damaged rope or a rope that has had to carry big loads during a rescue must be replaced.

> **Tip**
> The linear breaking load of a throw bag rope should be at least 1000 kg, or even better 1500 kg.

The Soca river in Slovenia is a paradise for paddlers of all skill levels

Technique

Getting into the boat

As long as you enter your boat in still water, you can use the paddle bridge. If the current in the eddy is too strong, or if there is no eddy at all, the best thing to do is to start right from the river bank. Push yourself off the bank with one hand, holding the paddle in the other, and make sure that your bow is pointing upstream during the whole procedure. Then move away from the bank in a large arc. Start with your bow pointing down river only in exceptional situations.

Make sure to push yourself off strongly if you are doing a cliff start

Rudder strokes

The faster the current gets, the quicker you have to react and turn your boat. In the following I will introduce you to a number of strokes which you should practice in flat water first.

The rudder stroke makes for a precise ferry

The reverse sweep stroke

For the reverse sweep stroke, you need to twist your torso towards the side of the stroke and dig the paddle in next to the stern. Keep looking at your active blade to give your torso the required pre-rotation. Keep the paddle shaft in front of your belly and make a wide arc away from the boat with the active blade, until it is level with your body.

The torso rotation is important, since you can hardly get enough power out of your arms for this stroke – they remain in the fairly static position of the paddle box. This technique can also be practiced well on land.

Stern rudder

If you are traversing a rapid or surfing a wave, you can use the initial part of the reverse sweep stroke, similar to the forward sweep stroke, as a rudder. In this case you don't carry out the complete stroke, but only the first third of it, and the oncoming current delivers enough resistance to cause a change in direction. Don't look back to your stern, but in the desired direction of travel.

> Tip

> For turning the boat on the spot, nothing beats the combination of a forward sweep stroke and a reverse sweep stroke on the opposite side.

a Dig your paddle in parallel to the boat and...

b ...make a wide arc away from the boat

C Finish the stroke in a neutral seating position

The bow rudder

The reverse sweep stroke is good for turning the boat without any forward movement. If you want to do a turn with a certain forward momentum, you do need a new stroke. The bow rudder helps you to turn the boat while you still keep it moving forward. The bow rudder might be one of the most difficult, but it is also one of the most important strokes! Since it allows an easy transition into a forward or sweep stroke, it offers you many different stroke combinations.

To practice it in flat water, start with a few strong forward strokes. Initiate a turn with a slight sweep stroke on your left, turn your torso to the right and take your left hand up in front of your head. The paddle should now be pointing down vertically from this hand, so you also need to tilt your torso sideways, as you would to edge the boat.

The active hand now opens the blade forward,

> Tip

> Adjust your blade position according to the pressure you feel, because this fine adjustment makes up at least 50% of your success.

> The bow rudder only works if you lean courageously into the turn, while keeping the boat flat, and only then can you set up the paddle vertically. In flat water the boat needs enough forward momentum to provide pressure for the paddle blade to stay on the surface.

a Get up speed

b Pre-rotate your upper body

c Move the boat around the paddle...

d ...and the paddle towards the boat

moving the front edge of the blade away from the bow. To do this both wrists now have to be bent backward, and at the same time the blade is moved forward and away from the boat. As soon as you feel that pressure has built up on your blade, pull your boat around the paddle shaft with your left knee. As for any other stroke techniques, the power for the bow rudder comes out of the torso – the upper body pre-rotates, the boat follows.

In the beginning you need some guts for the strong twisting and the wide lean the bow rudder requires. To help you – just imagine yourself running past a pole, grabbing it and swinging around it.

Bow rudder abstracted

Safety

Before you start a river run and before you enter a rapid, you need to check a list of questions concerning you and your personal safety.

– Does the chosen section or rapid meet my skills, my experience and my equipment?

– Am I physically and mentally strong enough to perform at my very best?

– Have I recognized and understood the up-coming dangers of this section?

– In the case of an accident, are my fellow paddlers, and myself, able to react appropriately?

White water paddling can be dangerous, even highly dangerous. So answer these questions honestly. In the case that something goes wrong, and this happens over and over again, you must know what to do. In the following you will find hints and techniques for handling the smaller or the bigger mishaps in white water paddling. Remember: Shit happens, at least twice a week!

The swim

"He who paddles little, swims little".
Hans Mayer.

Capsizing and leaving the boat, i.e. failing to roll, is precisely called "swimming", whereby swimming has a very bitter taste among paddlers. He who swims, he is a loser, and he has to shout at least one liter of beer for each of the rescuers!

Nevertheless, this has happened to everyone at some time, and will continue to happen as long as paddling exists. Mistakes have their origin in human nature, and learning from mistakes is tough but effective. Swimming in white water requires special techniques and has to be practiced regularly. The best white water swimming spot that I know is the Augsburg Eiskanal in Germany - on a hot August day.

> Tip

> If you swim in white water, always make sure to save your skin first – material always comes second. This goes for swimmers as well as for the rescuers.

Swimming in white water

– Let boat and paddle go! Only in exceptional situations, especially in big water or in big tow-backs, does it makes sense to stay with the boat and gasp for air.

– Orientate yourself, get into a belly down position and start swimming over-arm strongly towards the bank.

If you end up in a cataract in which you are unable to swim, observe the following:

– Swim on your back and stretch your legs out in front of you on the surface of the water, feet first. There are underwater rocks in which you can trap your legs and feet, and in a strong current it is mostly impossible to free them again. This poses a serious risk of drowning!

– Watch downriver and breathe while your head is on the surface – the smallest wave will wash over your head, so watch for them and adjust your breathing rhythm accordingly.

– In this swimming position you can push yourself off the rocks and in the desired direction. Once I even saw how a swimmer climbed onto a rock in the middle of the current and jumped over the pour-over behind it!

– If you have to swim over a waterfall, roll up into a ball to protect your extremities.

Passive swimming position with feet first

Throw bag rescue

A throw bag rescue should be a standard skill for every white water paddler, and it is necessary to be familiar with both roles: being the victim and the rescuer.

Victim:
As a victim you should know where the rescuers position is and try to make eye contact with him. If the throw bag comes flying at you, grab the rope with both hands in front of your chest and turn onto your back. This is how you stay on the surface and keep breathing once the rope starts pulling you in. Never ever wrap the rope around your wrist! It is important that you are able to let the rope go in case of emergency!

Rescuer:
Ideally, a rescue is prepared before the potential victim hits the rapid. As a rescuer, place yourself at the exit of the rapid. Only now does the victim have enough time to try rolling and to get out of the boat. Place yourself at a point from which you have the possibility of letting the victim on the rope swing into an eddy. For this you need to calculate the distance to the swimmer, plus a few meters of tolerance. These estimates can be very delicate – I once watched a rescuer swing the swimmer right in front of a dangerous siphon!

Prepare your throw bag and make sure that there is no carabiner fixed to the bag. Take about two meters of rope out of the bag, grab the bag with your throwing hand and the rope with the other. Only once you have eye contact with the swimmer, throw the bag beyond the victim.
As soon as the swimmer grabs the rope, be prepared for a strong pull – it is best to sit down and to brace yourself against the direction of the pull as soon as the swimmer grabs the rope. If there is a strong current, put the rope over your shoulder and let it go for a short instance with the first pull – this helps both of you since it dampens the drag on both ends of the rope.

Even though there is a lot of discussion about the right way to throw the bag, I think the so-called "shock throw" (underarm throw), is best suited for this flying object. In any case, it is necessary to constantly practice throwing the bag, even if you are a "pro".

a Make eye contact with the swimmer

b Throw beyond the swimmer

c Brace yourself at the bank

d The swimmer grabs the rope and turns onto his back

The second try

One thing can be really depressing – you plan a rescue, prepare everything, and look forward to your moment of glory as the indispensable rescuer. You get a secure stance, establish eye contact, aim carefully, and then miss the victim by a country mile. If you are lucky you might have enough time to recollect your rope and start sprinting along the river bank behind your victim, ready to try a second throw.

The deciding factor for a second throw is coiling the rope cleanly. Take the loops of rope and throw again – the bag and the loops together. Do not forget to keep a tight hold of the loose end!

If you are only throwing a short distance you will be quicker if you throw the loose end towards the swimmer.

Second throw with a coiled rope

Tip

> For a long second throw it is helpful to fill the empty bag with water to increase its weight.

> The handling of the throw bag also needs to be practiced. On a nice sunny day it can be as much fun to try out some rescue techniques, as paddling itself!

> Don't try to grab the bag if you are swimming, go for the rope instead! Sometimes there are still a few meters left in the bag, which prolong your rescue unnecessarily.

Rescue from the boat

Saving a swimmer

On an easy river you normally rescue a swimmer with the boat, since there is no actual need for setting up a rescue post. On a wide river this can also be your only choice.

In this case the person being rescued should grab the stern of the kayak and kick powerfully. If you are using a longer boat with large volume, it is even possible to climb onto the stern of the boat and hold the rim of the cockpit, stabilizing with both legs on the left and right.

The swimmer lies on the stern and holds onto the rim of the cockpit

Saving the boat and paddle

Getting boat and paddle to the bank in a strong current is a mission in its own right. To complement the perfect safety provided from the bank, you should also have paddlers on the river, waiting at the end of the rapid or section.

To retrieve a paddle, try to grip the stray paddle together with your own, and make your way to the bank paddling with both paddles held together. Alternatively, throw the paddle ashore, or at least into an eddy.

To save a boat, you have a number of different options: you can either push it towards the bank, or, more tricky, pull it with the cowtail. Never hook a boat up to your cowtail in blind or difficult white water. It is better then to hit the cockpit rim with your bow and try pushing it towards the bank where it can somehow get stuck between rocks. If the boat does not stay put, you will have to overtake it, jump out of your boat and try to catch the runaway boat as it comes past. Alternatively, you can have somebody else waiting at the bank to catch the boat as you push it in.

> Tip

> Especially when saving a boat or a paddle – only one piece of gear per person!

> Never risk anything for the rescue of material; material can be replaced! You cannot!

> If you have to rescue several pieces of gear or swimmers – always start with the one that is furthest downstream!

> Never hook up a boat which has no airbags!

Tactics and maneuvers

You can learn the following paddling techniques, just like the basic skills of the first chapter, in flat water. The tactics and maneuvers should then be practiced in moving water.

Eddy turns

You put the boat into the water and go – that's how every river trip starts. The maneuver out of the eddy and into the current is called eddying in. The eddy out maneuver brings you back from the current into the eddy. The generic term for these maneuvers is eddy turns.

These eddy turns will accompany you through your whole kayak career, and will remain the most important maneuvers of all. No matter whether you are touring down the local river, or if you have to stop and scout in a roaring cataract on the verge of a waterfall, you will be paddling eddy turns.

Eddying in

Start with you bow pointing upstream and take up speed towards the eddy line. Cross the eddy line with good forward momentum and at an angle of about 45°. As soon as your bow crosses the eddy line, edge the boat downstream and push it into the main current with a strong sweep stroke on the downriver side. Now lean downstream and onto a paddle brace. If the boat doesn't turn completely downstream you can support the turn with a reverse sweep out of this position.

Eddy turns are the most important maneuvers in white water

> Cross the eddy line with the greatest possible forward momentum. The stronger the eddy, the stronger the sweep stroke required to take you across the eddy line.

> The stronger the current, the more downstream lean is required (outrigging).

Start with good forward momentum – push yourself across the eddy line with a strong sweep – edge the boat downriver and stabilize it with a brace

Eddy out

The opposite to the eddy in is the eddy out. This move is actually even more important, since the eddy out move enables you to stop and exit the current before you reach danger areas.

Start heading for the eddy from well upstream. Get up speed, coming from the middle of the river, and paddle strongly towards the eddy line. In the beginning it is difficult to estimate the speed of the current, so it is necessary to try and hit the eddy in its upper third. Ideally you will shoot across the eddy line at an angle of 45°. As soon as your bow hits the eddy line, push yourself actively across the eddy line with a sweep stroke on the upstream side. Edge your boat upstream, and use the sweep stroke as a brace. Keep holding the edge and stabilize yourself with a brace. From this position you can easily turn the boat with a slight reverse sweep, in case you are approaching the bank too quickly.

> **Tip**

> Always try to get as far as possible "into" the eddy, in order to stay out of the turbulence on the eddy line.

> The „sweep" that pushes you across the eddy line is a hybrid of a sweep stroke and a stern rudder. It starts only slightly in front of your body (not at the bow), and is performed with outrigging towards the active side. At the end of the stroke, when you are in the stern rudder position, you can either push to aid or pull hinder the turning of the boat.

New School Eddy Turnz

A few years ago kayaks were almost twice as long and were extremely hard to maneuver. The old techniques dealt solely with the turning of the boat. When you did eddy turns with old boats, you often had to actively help the current, using a reverse sweep or bow rudder to turn the boat in the new direction. Today we use boats which are half as long, and which sometimes turn faster than we'd like them to. It is time for new techniques to keep the boat tracking.

When doing eddy turns, we have to work against the turning impulse of the current, in order to get across the turbulence of the eddy line. This means: when you eddy out or in, you have to push the boat across the eddy line with one stroke and keep it tracking with the tension of your body, before you "lead" it into the new direction. This sweep stroke is carried out on the downstream side for the eddy in, and on the upstream side for the eddy out.

Directing your gaze

Every novice fixes his gaze on his paddle, which is okay, and is certainly safe enough. If you are on white water, however, you must keep your eye on the river. The current moves swiftly, and an upcoming obstacle or problem must be recognized early enough.

If there is a passage through some rocks or past a tree, keep your eyes on the passage and not on the obstacle. This basic rule applies for paddling as well as for skiing and driving a car. It sounds banal, but it is a fundamental principle which must be followed!

If a sudden change of course is required, look immediately in the new direction. Firstly, this enables you to plot a new route, both physically and mentally. Secondly, your head will guide your torso with the rotation required to turn the boat, which is essential for draw or sweep strokes.

Choose your line from well upstream – push yourself across the eddy line with a strong stroke on the upstream side – edge – and stabilize with a brace

The ferry

Crossing a river without being carried downstream is called ferrying, and in white water this standard maneuver has numerous uses.

The ferry is one of the best exercises for practicing your edging, your eddy turning, or simply your understanding of currents. A difficult ferry will always be a challenge.

Find yourself two eddies on opposite sides of the river. Paddle out of one eddy, holding a slightly more acute angle (bow pointing further upstream) than for eddying in– the faster the current, the more acute the angle has to be, the more upstream your bow has to point! Assessing this angle properly is half the game, because if you do it right, the boat basically hits the other side by itself. The edging is more or less equivalent to the edging for eddy turns. Once you are in the current, edge slightly downstream until you reach the eddy on the other side.

For longer ferries you need to hold the angle by doing forward and sweep strokes. For shorter ferries simply use the paddle blade of the sweep stroke that pushed you across the eddy line as a stern rudder, leaving it in the water to maintain the boat's angle.

If your ferry angle is not acute enough, the boat will immediately turn downstream. Only if the current is not too strong will you then succeed in bringing the boat back on course with a few strong sweep strokes. If this does not work, keep the boat turning downstream and simply return to the eddy from which you just started.

If your ferry angle is too steep, the boat will stall "into the wind". This means that your bow points straight upstream, you lose all your forward momentum, and start to drift downstream with the current. Correct this with a sweep stroke which will turn you in the desired direction, followed by powerful paddling to get you where you want to go.

Accelerate out of the eddy at a steep angle into the main current – control the boat with a stern rudder – and head for the new eddy as usual

Paddling river bends

As with bends in motor sports, there is also an ideal line through river bends in white water. Tight bends form a pillow on the outside and an eddy on the inside. If you want to stay away from these turbulent zones you have to follow the main current close to the inside of the bend, and close to the eddy line.

The ideal line follows the inside of the bend

> Tip

> All these maneuvers sound simple and logical enough – but you will find out how many things can go wrong once you start practicing them. But relax in your boat, paddle with conviction, and don't try to fight against the water in the beginning.
> If your ferry angle is too "flat", your boat will veer away downstream and it makes no sense to paddle like berserk against the current. If this happens, simply turn full circle and paddle back into the eddy that you started from.
> In doing this you turn with the current, following the current with your boat and thus using the energy of the current. This makes much more sense than using all your energy to work against it!

Paddling also is an underwater sport

Head work

Swim and feel the current!

It is difficult for a novice to recognize and to understand currents. In a kayak you float on top of the water, and the current's effects on the movement of the boat are often delayed or only barely detectable. The best way to understand an eddy is to swim into one – that's how you really feel the difference between main current and eddy, and how much momentum it really takes to get across the eddy line. Again, the Eiskanal in Augsburg, or any other artificial white water run, is best suited for such exercises – no sharp rocks, and bath-temperature water!

Capsizing

During your first contacts with currents you will most certainly capsize now and then – no big deal, but a good reason to learn the Eskimo roll as soon as possible. With this skill in your bag of tricks you will learn to paddle quicker and easier. Not only will you save time and energy, but you will no longer be afraid of capsizing, so your mind will be free to focus on paddling.

Your learning environment is of great importance to your success. For example, the Soca river in Slovenia, or the Sesia in the Italian Piemonte, are rivers with crystal clear waters, in which even capsizing can be a lot of fun. It is no wonder that these are two of the most popular rivers for beginners in the whole Alps.

Tricks

The "shuttle"

You are on your way to the river, have found the put in and the take out on a map, and maybe even thought about how you get back to your car from the take out.

"Moving the car" is a central part of every river trip, even though it has nothing to do with paddling. Ideally you are traveling with two cars – then you can leave one car and dry clothing at the take out. If you only have one car it is nice to have a driver, a so-called "shuttle bunny". If not, you have to check for other options.

Hitchhiking might be the simplest solution, but on most of the tourist routes in the Alps, or in really remote valleys, it can take hours to get a lift. It is mostly locals who share rides. Here's my advice: always have some dry clothing at the take out, and wear colorful clothing that says: "I am a sportsman". Dry clothing can either be stored at the take out or be transported in the boat in a dry bag.

If you have the possibility of taking a bicycle along on your trips to the river, you can round off every paddling trip with a little bike ride back to the put in. But even a little jog back to the put in never did anyone any harm, depending on the distance and the state the paddlers are in after the river trip!

On a few rivers you can use public transport for the shuttle, and on the Vorderrhein in Switzerland and the Koppentraun in Austria it is even possible to take your boats along in the train.

On the West Coast of New Zealand aeronautic means of transportation are an absolute necessity

Whitewater
and your senses

Control in white water is achieved by recognizing and immediately reacting to the slightest impulses – but a rapid response is only possible as long as your paddle blade is in the water.

As a novice you will often be surprised by currents. See the paddle as an extension of your arms, and the paddle can deliver information about currents that you don't see at first glance.

White water paddling blows your mind – a feast for the senses!

Getting used to the boat and body tension

For successful learning it is necessary to become familiar with the muscles that move the boat, and to control them consciously. For this it is essential to know that the paddle forms a stable anchor point in the water, that the boat is the mobile element, and that the torso and arm muscles transmit the motion. Assuming that your arms are in an almost static position in the paddle box, your boat is moved mainly by your torso muscles.

With this in mind, you can simulate the motions of the paddle and the boat with a table and an office chair on wheels. With your hands holding on to the table, keep your feet up and roll the chair back and forth, and from side to side. Concentrate on the muscles that you are using to roll the chair. You will realize pretty soon that your torso muscles play the major role in the movement of the chair – and these are the same muscles that you use to move your boat. Now that you can feel which muscles are

required to move the boat/chair, you can put them to good use!

Correct seating posture (p.23) is a prerequisite for the active work of the torso muscles, and the second concept you need to grasp here. It is definitely one of the most difficult and important learning steps to maintain this basic position and the body tension, and to never lose control over your boat, no matter what happens.

The Grand Canyon de Verdon is the most impressive gorge in Europe

In the gorges of the Inn river

Reading and understanding white water. Combat paddling

White water; class 2-3

Hear the call of the white water! As soon as you are familiar with the techniques and maneuvers of the previous chapters, you are ready to go for your first experiences in waves, holes and cataracts. But beware, beginners tend to forget about the basics pretty quickly. If you are technically out of your depth in white water, you won't be able to learn anything about understanding the current.

Class 2 - 3 white water combines many different forms of currents, nevertheless you are playing on fairly safe terrain. Here you will gain experience with currents, waves, holes and cataracts. Only when you understand white water can you learn to appraise it and be able to develop a tactic for running a section or a rapid safely.

Big water and creeks

From class 3 white water onwards we differentiate between two types of rivers:

Big water stands for large volume rivers with comparatively few technical difficulties and gradient. The difficulties arise due to the high speed of the current, and large waves and holes.
Creeks offer highly technical and steep white water. They are characterized by steep gradient and high drops. The difficulties entail complicated lines and the resulting greater technical demands on the paddler.

High volume, technical white water quickly approaches the limit of navigability.

Class 2: moderately difficult

Water: irregular course of current, irregular waves, holes, whirlpools and pillows

Riverbed: few obstacles in the main current, small ledges

Class 3: difficult

Water: high, irregular waves, longer wave-trains, holes, whirlpools and pillows

Riverbed: isolated boulders, ledges, other obstacles in the main current

class 2 Saalach river, Austria

class 3 Middle section of the Verzasca rive

White water anatomy

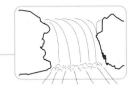

So far we have considered currents as flat, two dimensional areas. On a class 2-3 river this is no longer sufficient. Waves and holes are three dimensional objects. To assess and to ride them also requires, next to a little balance, some knowledge about their make-up and their origin.

Waves

A huge wave train is a paddler's paradise. As in a roller coaster, the waves can throw you around without being a real danger. A fat wave train will blow your mind over and over again, letting you inside the heart of the river, letting you feel its sheer power.

Waves are caused by the water's urge to level itself out. If water falls over an obstacle, it accelerates towards the bottom of the riverbed and forms a wave by then shooting back up and leveling out.

If the water shoots up very steeply (almost vertically) after an obstacle, it also gets slowed down by gravity. That's how the foam pile of a so-called breaking wave forms.

Waves can form as the result of many different kinds of obstacles in the river bed: rocks or ledges on the bottom, or tight spots which first dam the water and then cause it to accelerate strongly. A classic wave train forms its biggest wave upstream, at the beginning, and the waves then grow progressively smaller.

Waves can also have their origin in tidal rapids. Skookumchuk Narrows, BC

Foam pile

Green wave

Seen from a bird's eye view, the waves of a wave train form a V which opens upstream. In the middle of the current the river is as its deepest, has its fastest flowing water, and the waves are the highest. In a wave train, the mid section of the V is normally the best course to follow.

The "V"

In technical cataracts small V's often form between the rocks. In most cases, the best way through can also be found in the fastest and deepest current, at the apex of the V.

Peak

Face

Trough

Hole

A strongly breaking wave is called a hole, and is characterized by the foam pile which is constantly falling back into the trough.

The stronger the foam is falling or streaming upstream, the more it can slow down or even hold a paddler. Big holes can grow to a height of several meters. Surfing a broken wave in the sea also equates to riding a hole in a river.

Waves and holes can have countless different forms – they are the "salt in your white water soup". Waves are fairly easy to paddle, whereas holes are considerably more difficult to handle. A hole which is on an angle to the main current can shoot a paddler a few meters sideways in the blink of an eye. And a strong back tow can hold a paddler or even a swimmer for an unpleasant, even dangerous length of time.

For your choice of route through a hole, the previously mentioned V again plays a major role. As with a wave, the tip of the V, which is the part of the hole furthest downstream, offers the best chance of a clean run through.

Back tow   Exit   Height

> Tip

> The highest waves mostly indicate the best route.

> Generally speaking, the stronger the foam pile, and the more water flowing back upstream, the more dangerous the hole.

> So: "Follow the V and you'll be free!

75

Back tows

The back tow is a particular kind of hole. A back tow forms when green water flows steeply over an obstacle and disappears deep in the riverbed. Smaller back tows are also known as pour-overs. A boil emerges where the current resurfaces, and from there the water flows almost horizontally back upstream. The size of a back tow is determined by the length of the stretch of water flowing back upstream from the boil. Dangerous back tows, which are difficult to get over, can be found especially behind so-called box weirs.

If the water is flowing back strongly for more than a meter, attempting to cross it in a boat can be critical. However, if the water is only flowing back moderately or gently, it can be possible to paddle through back tows of a few meters in length, under certain conditions. The strength and speed of a back tow is therefore just as important a factor as its length.

The best technique for running a back tow is a boof (see p. 122). If you paddle steeply off a drop and submerge your bow, your boat exposes a large surface area to the current of the back tow, and it is easily caught and held. Only if you keep your boat flat on the surface can you get up and maintain enough speed to shoot over the back tow.

The magic V

White water paddling means much more than just conquering a river, more than just steering your boat through some rapids. In a river landscape, away from all the social rules, a paddler follows his own ideals.

The phenomenon of following the V, the deepest and the fastest water, is for many paddlers more than just a successful paddling tactic – it has taken on somewhat of a cult status.

If it is not possible to follow the V for any reason – a lack of technique, fear, or if the main line simply can't be paddled – you can often take the so-called "chicken line", or the "sneak". Although this can sometimes be the wisest option, leaving the main current always smacks of cheating, and leaves a bitter taste in any paddler's mouth.

At the beginning of the nineties, the German Arnd Schaeftlein earned the reputation of being "Mr. Action Line". Even in the most challenging cataracts he simply nailed the main line every time, and he is still known worldwide as one of the best, most extreme and most fearless paddlers of his time.

Weirs

Once you are capable of assessing back tows, you can also judge weirs much better. But again: weirs are no white water. They either dam water for hydro power plants or they tame a river and lessen its gradient. Since in most valleys houses are built fairly close to the river, this technique is used to prevent the river from breaking its banks at high water levels. Paddlers should hold weirs in contempt. Weirs are nothing less than concrete constructions, imposed on a natural river landscape by men. They hold many dangers such as hidden steel or rotten wood constructions, and hazardous back tows. Such a back tow can often appear harmless, especially to a novice.
However, despite all skepticism: Not every weir is dangerous, and it can be fun to run it.

> Tip

> Golden rule for all weirs: if in doubt, portage!

Weir types

Box weir:

– often with strong back tow

Slide weir:

– strong back tow at high water levels

Boulder weir:

– the individual boulders are often con-nected with steel cables, posing a danger to both swimmers and paddlers

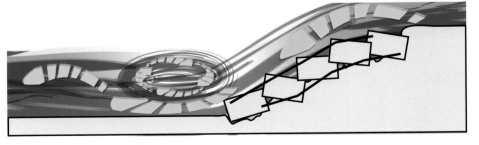

Pillow Rock,
Futaleufu, Chile

Pillows

When the water flows against a rock or the
bank on the outside of a river bend, a so-called
pillow is formed, which can be quite similar to
a hole or breaking wave; the water hitting the
rock flows back upstream in the form of a
foam pile.

Be extremely careful if there is no pillow building up in front of a rock or a wall – this means
that the space underneath is either hollow or
undercut, and can form a dangerous undertow.

Undercut right next to the route. Corran Addison
on the Sorba river, Italy

Seams and eddy lines

When two strong currents from different directions meet, a seam emerges. The flatter the angle between the two currents is, the stronger the seam is. The strongest seams can be found at eddy lines (angle = 180°). Whirlpools form along strong seams, sucking down both water and air. On big rivers you can find whirlpools with a diameter of a few meters which are able to submerge a paddler with his boat. But whirlpools of this size are fairly rare, most are only a few centimeters in diameter, and are hardly visible on the eddy line.

Boils

Boils can be found after waterfalls, undercuts, siphons or whirlpools. They occur in any situation where a current is reflected off the bottom of the river and returned to the surface.

Boulder gardens and cataracts

Add a few boulders to a wave train, and you have yourself a cataract – a rapid interspersed with rocks. A cataract consists of all above mentioned forms of currents – pillows in front of rocks, eddies immediately behind, and waves and holes in between. A steep cataract always presents a challenge for a paddler, since he has to plan a line and avoid the obstacles.

Cataracts and boulder gardens exist in countless different forms: with large boulders or little rocks, tight passages or wide passages, steep or low gradient, long or short sections. The difficulty of a cataract is always influenced by the above mentioned factors.

The more rocks there are in the current, the slower the river gets – the gradient does not have a linear drop, but is broken into steps. As with weirs, these steps slow the river down, and as a consequence you find pools and eddies after the passages.

In a cataract you can also learn how to handle rocks, and to see them not only as obstacles, but as points of orientation.

The Inn river in Switzerland offers a wide variety of different types of white water

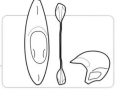

Gear

The Boat

For a white water novice, it is recommendable to use a boat which tracks well, and which has a length of 2.30 - 2.80 meters. It should not have too much volume (200 –270 liters). Such a boat will be stable enough to allow you to learn safely, developing your skills and techniques to an advanced level, while still being reactive enough to give you a feeling for currents and the moving water.

Equipment

The equipment for moving water and for white water is pretty much the same, but be prepared; on a cold mountain river, with its waves and holes, you are as much underwater as on the surface, and good equipment increases both the fun and the safety factor.

Finstermuenz Gorge of the Inn river, Switzerland

Technique

Stabilizing

Balance is the fundamental prerequisite for controlled paddling – as long as you have to brace you are unable to steer.

A flexible lumbar area is the key to action and reaction in turbulent white water. It is the kayaker's central pivot point, connecting the static lower part of the body with the dynamic upper body.

In order to achieve the optimal position for your lumbar vertebrae it is necessary to always sit forward on your buttocks, and to not lean against the back rest. Keep your back straight and your upper body leaning slightly forward. Your thighs should be firmly fitted into the thigh braces, with the balls of your feet pressed against the foot rests. If your arms are now slightly bent, the paddle held in a low position, and your stomach muscles are tensed, you are ready to do some serious paddling.

In this position you can quickly paddle forward, brace, edge, boof and roll – everything happens in a flash, and is carried out with maximum efficiency.

Active combat paddling

In a lot of white water situations attack is the best defense. The combination of optimal seating position and active paddling is therefore called "combat paddling". This combat position should become the expression of your aggressive yet positive state of mind.

If you are going for a challenging rapid, let it rock! Lean your upper body forward and keep paddling continuously. The resulting speed not only leads to greater safety through increased boat stability, but the strokes themselves also stabilize you. The next wave is your target.

Once you reach it, aim straight for the next one. The combat position is completely useless if you give up your body tension and lean back at the first sign of turbulence. Leaning back is not only an ergonomic disaster, but psychologically seen, you are also putting yourself into a submissive "loser's pose". That's why you throw yourself against any oncoming waves or holes with all your might, and show them who is boss! Big time! This attacking of the waves also has other advantages: your paddle remains in the water and you can immediately carry out small corrective moves. Even if you capsize, you are already leaning forward and can roll right away.

> **Tip**

> If you are heading for an exciting rapid, the combat position should give expression to your optimistic-aggressive state of mind.
> Don't forget: you are a machine!

...**O**laf Obsommer knows what he is doing

Stroke combinations

An expert guides, steers, accelerates, stabilizes and boofs his boat without taking the paddle out of the water. To attain such virtuoso paddling technique, superbly combining the different strokes – this is the art of paddling.

Basics

The paddle is your rudder. As long it is in the water, you have control. Stroke combinations are quite tricky in the beginning, since the paddle tends to cut under. However, you can develop the required fine touch for the paddle with the following exercises:

1.Turn the boat on the spot with bow rudders, practicing with the right blade to turn you clockwise, and the left blade counter clockwise.

a Initiate a turn with a bow rudder...

b ...until the paddle is next to the bow

c Take your paddle back along the boat until it is behind your body

d Begin the next bow rudder

a Initiate a turn with a sweep stroke...

b ...until the paddle is next to the stern

c Bring your paddle forward along the boat until it is in front of you

d Begin the next sweep stroke

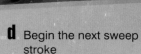

Keep the blade in the water, and move it as follows:
Perform the first bow rudder, pulling the boat to the paddle. As soon as the paddle reaches the boat (at about knee level), with the face of the paddle towards the boat, draw the paddle down the length of the boat until it is next to your upper body. Then open the blade angle and push the paddle away from the boat to initiate the next bow rudder. Keep repeating the movement so that the boat turns smoothly and continuously. Then practice on the other side.

2. Turn the boat on the spot using sweep strokes, with the left blade turning the boat clockwise and the right one counter clockwise. Keep the blade in the water, and move it as follows:
As soon as the paddle has reached the boat behind your body after the first sweep stroke, push the paddle forward again, with the face towards your body – into the starting position. Perform the next sweep stroke.

Practice on both the left and the right side, until you master the two variants without cutting under.

The combination of draw- and forward stroke

This combination is one of the most important techniques for new school paddlers, because it allows you to not only turn the boat, but also to accelerate it into a new direction.
It is used for anything from paddling out of an eddy into the current, to the last minute correction as you boof off the edge of a monster waterfall.

To practice this combination of strokes on flat water, you should start with the exercise for the bow rudder. As soon as the pressure on the blade lessens as the blade reaches the boat, turn the blade to face back and pull it strongly along the boat – like a forward stroke with a vertical shaft – until your action arm is bent 90° and your upper body is upright.

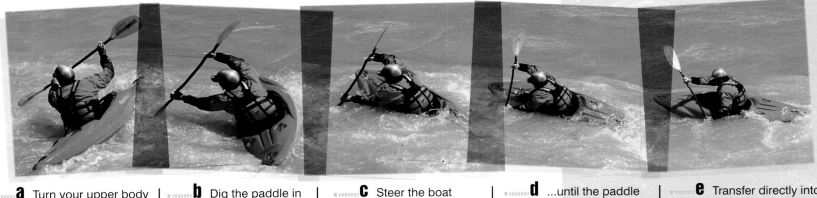

a Turn your upper body into the new direction

b Dig the paddle in vertically

c Steer the boat around the paddle...

d ...until the paddle touches the boat

e Transfer directly into a forward stroke

Shifting the boat sideways

In technical, as well as in big water, you often have to shift your boat a few meters sideways in order to avoid an obstacle. In white water the current can move so quickly that the technique we have used until now – turning the boat then paddling forward – would pretty soon get us into a world of trouble. We need a new technique, pronto!

Basically there are two stroke combinations which are well suited to this: the S-stroke and the draw stroke.

The S-stroke

The S-stroke is very helpful in big water, when the boat has a decent forward speed.

While moving forward you turn the boat in the new direction with a bow rudder. Without taking the paddle out of the water, you transit directly into a forward stroke, holding the shaft as steeply as possible. Only pull the forward stroke as far as your knee and finish this combination with a strong sweep stroke.

Sure, the S-stroke as described above only shifts the boat sideways a small distance, since you're really just doing a long S-turn. However, it has the advantage that the boat keeps its forward momentum. This is the reason why this stroke is very often seen in kayak slalom.

> **Tip**

> The S-stroke is perfect for shooting through an eddy in the center of the river, without losing speed.

a Turn the boat with a bow rudder, going fast forward

b The initiation of the forward stroke keeps the boat "going"

c Bring your opposite hand up to your chest

d Finish with a sweep stroke

The draw stroke

Especially in steep and technical whitewater, you don't have very much forward momentum. Pretty often, you will approach cataracts slowly, or even paddling backwards, to catch a glimpse over the ledge and to scout the route. In case you have to shift your boat sideways in the last second to hit the perfect line, a draw stroke or an upstream backward ferry are the right technique.

Hold the paddle as steep as for a bow rudder, but dig it into the water sideways of your body with a straight active arm and as far away from the boat as possible. Make sure that your weight remains over the boat and start pulling towards your body. Get the blade out of the water, turning it into a forward stroke position,

in the second before the paddle hits the boat, because otherwise you can capsize yourself, big time. You can repeat this stroke as often as you want or have to.

> **Tip**
>
> The secret of the draw stroke is to take the paddle out of the water in time. As soon as your blade hits the boat, you turn yourself upside down with the leverage of the paddle.

a Keep the paddle in a steep position and dig it into the water next to you

b Don't pull the paddle all the way towards the boat

c Take the paddle completely out of the water

d Repeat the stroke as often as needed

Riding holes and pillows

Holes

The exciting and challenging thing about white water paddling is that shit happens, all the time! For unforeseeable situations there are a bunch of emergency techniques. One of them is riding a hole, and leaving it while staying under control.

If a boat gets stuck in a hole, it will sooner or later be pushed into a side surf position by the foam pile of the hole.

If you are able to control this side surf, you can work yourself to the sides of the hole with a few forward strokes and exit. The basic position for hole riding is almost identical with the white water combat position – upper body bent slightly forward, stomach muscles tense, but still relaxed around your hip. To avoid an upstream capsize during your turbulent ride in the hole, it is necessary to shift your weight onto your downstream buttock and to edge downstream. Use a downstream brace to stabilize this position, but you should try to put as little weight as possible on the paddle. If you want to get out of the hole, choose the exit which is further downstream. Using strong forwards or backwards strokes you should soon reach the exit. Make sure that you dig your paddle in as far forward or backward as possible to ensure long and efficient strokes. Ideally, you should balance the boat with your hip only, you don't have to brace, and can concentrate on paddling hard forward or backward. Another tricky thing about holes is that their exits often hold particularly strongly. Paddle as hard as possible to break out and get your boat out completely.
If the exit is too strong to escape, surf back to the other end of the hole and try to shoot towards the exit with maximum speed.

In weaker holes, which you would also ride for tactical reasons, you can use the so-called "exit stroke". For this you keep the paddle next to your thigh and deep in the green water, with

> **Tip**

> Also use holes to stop, or to traverse intentionally.

Relax – the golden rule for hole riding

Doing strong forward strokes can get you out of almost any hole the shaft vertical, as if doing a forward stroke. Now turn the active blade towards your stern, the face of the paddle facing diagonally to the main current and the boat all of a sudden starts moving forward.

The exit stroke is a very stable because it is a static stroke and it has a very strong bracing effect.

Exit of a hole

Side surfing pillows

Riding pillows and holes can be an emergency technique, or can be intentionally integrated into the desired route. A fat pillow has a lot in common with a hole. If you are drifting sideways towards a rock which only has a small cushion, it is almost impossible to avoid contact with the rock. Prepare for such an impact in the combat position – upper body in a slight forward lean, legs tightly squeezed into the boat and the paddle ready for bracing towards the obstacle. Now the current cannot catch your upper deck and cause you to capsize. Brace on the rock with the paddle or your hand and actively push yourself around the obstacle.

Brace courageously towards the rock

> **Tip**

> The stronger the current pushes you sideways towards a rock, the more you have to lean into the direction of the obstacle.

Pivot turn

The fastest way to turn your boat is a pivot turn and every serious paddler should have this technique in his bag of tricks. For this move, you cut your stern under the waterline with a backward sweep stroke and turn it around your body, on the spot. The only condition is that you need a boat with a low volume stern.

To get the stern under the surface, you have to edge your boat on the opposite side of the stroke, and twist your upper body in the direction of the turn. Since this whole thing is very delicate, it pays to start practicing on flat water first.

Take up speed with a few hard forward strokes, turn your torso to one side and edge your boat to the other. You will only get your stern under if you twist your upper body in a sudden jerk with a corresponding edging of the boat. Look to your stern, dig the paddle into the water next to it and do a powerful backward sweep stroke, turning the boat around your body. As soon as the turning movement starts, edge back and keep the boat turning flat; your goal is to cut the stern only a little under the surface.

This maneuver is made all the more elegant if you switch straight into a combination of a bow rudder and forward stroke right after you sink your stern, and thus accelerate the boat in the new direction.

a Turn your upper body towards the active side

b Edge to the opposite side and do a backward sweep stroke

c Shift straight into a bow rudder...

d ...and pull into a powerful forward stroke

The high brace

In white water you are constantly confronted with situations where you really don't want to capsize! If a low brace does not work for any reason, follow it up with a high brace.

Just like the low brace, you should practice the high brace at the bank first – sitting and without a boat. The movement of the upper body, the "C to C", is the same as for the low brace, and only your grasp of the paddle is different.

Shift your weight onto one buttock and let yourself fall over to one side. Bend your upper body away from the ground, as if you would do for edging the boat.

Bring your elbows down for bracing and catch yourself with the paddle, the face of the blade pointing down. Now you are "hanging" on the shaft. Avoid holding your paddle higher then your nose and keep the passive hand in front of your upper shoulder. The elbow of the passive side is tight against your upper body, to keep the paddle as flat on the water as possible, thereby providing maximum flotation for the blade.

To recover, pull yourself up with the paddle and flick your hips explosively to the other side, shifting your weight back onto both buttocks. Follow with your upper body and head last. On the water your paddle normally sinks very quickly, and the deeper it sinks into the water, the harder it gets to push yourself up. The only thing that helps is an explosive bracing technique and good timing.

> Tip

> Experts do not pull straight down on the paddle, but brace with a slight sweep stroke. Thus, the paddle produces more flotation, making the high brace bombproof.

a If you fall to the right bend your upper body to the left

b Brace explosively

c Bring your head back over the boat last

In order to practice and fine tune your high brace, learn to "hold your lean" in flat water. With a constant sculling motion of your paddle, keep the active blade on the surface and generate pressure, keeping you afloat.

Catch yourself on the water with a high brace and remain in this outrigging position, pushing the paddle towards the bow, and drawing it back again. The paddle will stay on the surface if you open the face of the blade towards your bow for the forward movement, and towards the stern for the backward movement.

Bracing with a sculling brace

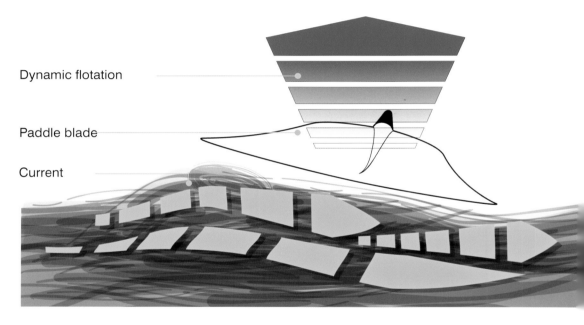

Dynamic flotation

Paddle blade

Current

> **Tip**

> A badly performed high brace is an acute danger for your shoulder joint – avoid it by keeping the elbow of the passive side tight to your body, and by never fully stretching the active arm.

> The sudden change from a low to a high brace is the rescue parachute of extreme white water pilots.

New boats, new techniques

It is very interesting to compare the advantages and disadvantages of old and new boat designs, and then deduce the necessity of different paddling techniques from this technical standpoint. Generally you have to differentiate between two design principles: Long, narrow and with a round bottom (old), or compact, wide and with a flat bottom (new). A long, narrow boat with a round bottom is fast, has good tracking, is relatively unaffected by cross currents, but is unstable and very hard to maneuver. If you paddle such a boat, you are mostly occupied with trying to get it around tight corners, thereby using a lot of energy and technique. You rarely have time to profit from its acceleration and its potential speed.

A short, wide boat with a flat bottom, on the other hand, is a lot easier to maneuver, floats high on the surface and, if paddled properly, hardly ever submerges. Nevertheless it is slow, loses speed instantly, tracks badly, and is sensitive to cross currents. A great advantage of flat bottom boats is their initial stability, lying on the water like a board. Thus you have a lot more time for paddling, instead of rolling and bracing. But a modern boat has to be faster than the current in demanding white water to really outperform the old designs, and this means one thing: you have to accelerate your boat with great efficiency and choose a line where you can keep your speed.

Techniques which keep the boat tracking are becoming more important than techniques for turning it.

When a boat is accelerated with a forward stroke, a turning impulse is also generated. The shorter the boat, the faster this impulse is transferred into a turning of the whole boat. Modern stroke combinations, which either turn the boat or bring it into a new direction of travel, make use of this effect.

Make sure to use your edges consciously; you can thus let cross currents pass under your boat, improving tracking or simplifying turns.

Safety

Water can be brutal and merciless. 10 cubic meters of water per second on a white water river equate to 10 tons of mass that are roaring downstream every second. The only way for us to control this enormous power is to stay on the surface. When you have to rescue a boat stuck against a rock below the water line, it quickly becomes frighteningly clear what sort of forces have to be reckoned with. The boat can be flattened like a pancake in a matter of seconds.

The greater the difficulties on a river, the more you must be aware of factors concerning safety and rescue. In a dangerous situation, the measures necessary for a rapid rescue should run like clockwork. Never stop practicing with the throw bag and working on simulated white water accidents, because in real life, every second counts.

Olli caught the Big One!

The leader of the rescue

If a human life is endangered you have to react spontaneously, but as a team, and totally rationally. Individual panic reactions lead to chaos and are of no help to the victim. As a consequence it is necessary that one member of the rescue group coordinates everything and allocates duties to the rest of the team.

The cowtail

The cowtail was actually developed to rescue an unconscious swimmer, but in most cases it is used to tow abandoned boats out of the water. But beware! Never use the cowtail if the further course of the river is obstructed or, even worse, unknown to you. Ending up in a difficult rapid with a hooked up boat is something you definitely want to avoid.
No matter what you have hooked, be it man or

boat, always head straight for the bank. Turn your boat downstream and look for a big safe eddy. It is a lot harder to cross the eddy line or to paddle in any direction at all due to the extra weight you are pulling along, so always check the course of the river ahead! Once you have reached the bank, make sure you have a spot where you can hold on to something, because the hooked up boat often remains in the current, and can try to pull you out again. Keep your paddle in reach, exit, pull your boat out first, and then the one behind you.
Normally you can rescue a boat a lot more quickly and efficiently if you simply point your bow into its cockpit and push it ashore with a ferry.

Your cowtail can also help if you get pinned in your boat; you can connect the cowtail to a rope thrown to you from the bank, and thus simplify the rescue. Especially in the case of a vertical pin it is helpful to have a rope pulling upstream against the push of the current to aid a safe exit from the boat.

The cowtail should always be well stowed, with no loose ends hanging out, as there are so many objects on a river in which you can get caught – if not on the water, then on the bank when scouting a rapid.

Save your souls!

This goes for any hairy situation in white water: man first, gear second! If you are swimming on a class 1 or 2 river it makes sense to grab your gear and try and get it to the bank. From class 3 onwards it is too dangerous – forget your gear, get yourself to the bank first, and then see what can be done to rescue the equipment.

Rope and pulley systems

Every white water paddler should be familiar with the rope and pulley technique, and have the required material in his boat. It is simply the best way to get a stuck boat out of the current.

A good alternative to a pulley system is to have all the members of the group pulling on the same line. Although the pulling forces are not as great as with a rope and pulley, a collective pulling effort is a lot faster to set up, and not as limiting when it comes to the direction in which you can pull.

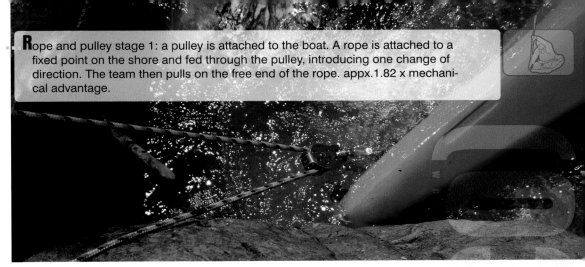

Rope and pulley stage 1: a pulley is attached to the boat. A rope is attached to a fixed point on the shore and fed through the pulley, introducing one change of direction. The team then pulls on the free end of the rope. appx.1.82 x mechanical advantage.

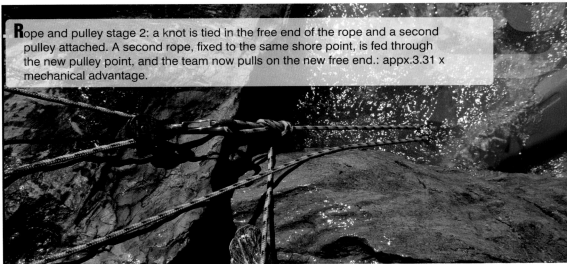

Rope and pulley stage 2: a knot is tied in the free end of the rope and a second pulley attached. A second rope, fixed to the same shore point, is fed through the new pulley point, and the team now pulls on the new free end.: appx.3.31 x mechanical advantage.

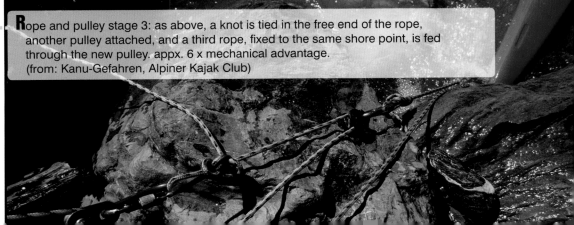

Rope and pulley stage 3: as above, a knot is tied in the free end of the rope, another pulley attached, and a third rope, fixed to the same shore point, is fed through the new pulley. appx. 6 x mechanical advantage.
(from: Kanu-Gefahren, Alpiner Kajak Club)

Double the hands make for half the work

> Golden Rule for all rescues – man comes before gear! Holds for rescuers and victims alike!

> With abrupt tugs on the rope you can often free a trapped boat.

Back tow rescue and swimming

Rescuing a swimmer out of a weir or a natural drop is always a critical situation.
The swimmer gets pushed into the falling water by the back tow and disappears under water. In this highly oxygenated water it takes a long time until the swimmer reappears at the surface.
A drop with a big back tow must be secured by at least a two man throw bag team on the bank and a paddler in a boat right behind the drop.

Back tow rescue

If a paddler cannot escape from a back tow on his own, it is necessary that rescuers intervene before he leaves the boat, and ideally that they throw the bag while he is on the surface and has eye contact.
If the paddler leaves the boat before you are able to throw the bag, try to throw it while he is on the surface, whether you have eye contact or not! If the swimmer has lost consciousness, or his orientation, it is necessary that a rescuer attached to a rope jump in the back tow and grab the swimmer. The rope should be attached to the rescue belt on the rescuer's life jacket. Now both have to be hauled out of the back tow at the same time, and swung into the safety of an eddy. Never underestimate the forces which are at work on a rope in such a situation.

As no two rescues are alike, every situation demands good judgment and spontaneous decisions.

Throw the rope before the paddler is exhausted!

Throw between boat and body!

As soon as the paddler grips the rope, start to p...

Pull him into a safe spot

Another happy ending – good Karma!

Swimming in a back tow

If you have to swim in a back tow it doesn't make sense to start swimming downriver. The best way out is to dive through the bottom of the hole, along with the falling water. Therefore you have to swim back upstream into the falling water and let yourself get dragged down as deep as possible. When you start going down roll up into a ball to protect your extremities. Normally you lose your orientation pretty quickly, so don't panic. Conserve your oxygen and check for rescuers and the rope. Sometimes the only way out of a natural tow back can be an exit at the side of the hole. If it exists, swim for it like your life depends on it. This could be the case!

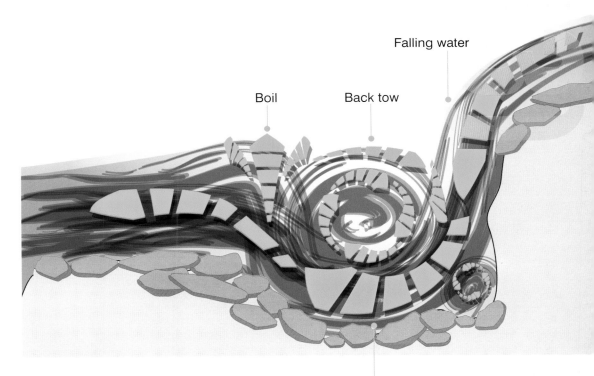

Falling water

Boil   Back tow

Bottom current

> **Tip**

> Critical or dangerous back tows must be scouted, and then paddled one by one. The rest of the crew secures the site from the bank and in boats.

> If you are the pitcher, stand downstream of the tow back.

> Always try to throw the rope before the paddler leaves the boat!

Eddy turn in the Lofer gorge, Austria

Tactics and maneuvers

Choosing the right river trip

At the beginning of your career, an unforgettable day's paddling is determined by your choice of the right white water run. If you look through river guide books or join up with some experienced paddlers, you will find loads of class 2 - 3 rivers to paddle. An ideal run for a class 2 - 3 novice is a run with some class 3 rapids, quiet pools in between, and lots of eddies to practice in. In the beginning stay away from runs which have long cataracts and few eddies. The same goes for runs with gorges and canyons which have no access from the bank – only paddle them once you feel completely confident paddling the difficulties described. Furthermore, you should try to gain experience on different types of white water and go for both big as well as technical white water at your particular level.

Stopping in front of obstacles

Class 3 white water is characterized by open passages, and normally you can spot your line from the boat.
Nonetheless, it makes sense to scout such a class 3 rapid – just imagine there is a tree stuck in the middle of the rapid, or a weir is located right behind it. Don't risk anything, check the details and the last eddy before the weir from the bank, before entering the rapid in your boat.

If the river follows a bend, the inside of the bend is better for scouting. If you start your run on the inside of the bend you can easily move to the outside if necessary. If you start on the outside, it can be impossible to make your way in if you need to.

Sometimes the outside of the bend is best for scouting if you expect to run the outer line, especially if the line is difficult to see from the inside, if the inner bank is not accessible, or if the river is follows an S-bend. Scouting an S-bend from the outside allows you to see into the upcoming rapid as well.

If the approach to the rapid is straight, scout the river on the side which is closer to the line which you intend to run, usually where the main current is. It is the job of the first paddler in the group to find a suitable eddy to stop in, and to guide the rest of the group in there.

To look at a rapid, analyze it, and then plan its run; this is one of the most important skills of a white water paddler. Even if a class 3 rapid can be paddled "on sight", a successful run, after previous scouting and planning of your line, gives you good feedback about your abilities to assess white water.

Scouting

A rapid always gets analyzed following the same procedure:

analyze, structure, recapitulate

First walk the length of the rapid and get an overview of danger spots and possible routes. When walking back upstream, link the separate sections and rapids together into one line, and try to memorize points of orientation as they will be seen from the boat. Points of orientation can be rocks, holes or other features on the river. When you put in you should have in your mind's eye a complete picture of the white water ahead of you, and your line through it.

The Lavertezzo Waterfall on the Verzasca, Switzerland

Tips for choosing a line:

- Always follow the biggest V's.
- Choose the straightest line possible.
- Give danger spots a wide berth.
- The current always pulls you into the outside of a bend, so cut the corners!

> Tip

> If your river guide book indicates unrunnable sections, check for possible exit points from the bank, before you begin the run.

> Always take a throw bag along when scouting a rapid – if you need to secure the section, you won't have to run back to get it

> Don't get into your boat until you have memorized the whole run, and can visualize it with closed eyes from a paddling perspective.

Read and run

The possible lines through a cataract on a class 2-3 section are visible from the boat, due to the river's moderate gradient.

Even if choosing a line seems to be easy, you should try to interpret and predict all the different currents you'll encounter from upstream, before you enter your boat. By doing this you gain valuable experience which helps you to run more and more difficult white water "on sight".

On difficult white water there are two deciding factors which dictate whether you can run a rapid on site, or whether it requires scouting: gradient and character of the river. After the first rapids of a run, you can usually get a reasonable feel for its character – are you confronted with mean sections and few eddies, trees in the current and strong back tows? Get scouting! Or are you welcomed by loads of eddies, deep pools and smooth, polished rocks? Can be largely paddled on site.

Checklist:
– Can I assess the course, gradient and thus the difficulty of the rapid?

If no:
– Where is the next tactically suitable eddy to scout or to portage from?

If yes:
– Where does the main current go, and does it look boatable?

If no:
– Is there another possible line?

Guiding a group

White water paddling is both an individual and a team sport. Everybody is responsible for his own actions, but nobody should ever endanger any of his fellow paddlers. The guy who paddles first, or leads the group, has a little more responsibility towards his companions. He always has to have an eye on all the others, assess their skills and keep them together. For example, he paddles into tactically important eddies and informs the rest of the group about the further course of the river. It is the most experienced paddler or the one who knows the river best who should guide. A democratic and homogenous group, in which all paddlers have the same skill level, will always have a spearhead paddler, even if they rotate after every rapid. The other paddlers of the group are also obliged to do their part in keeping the group together, to not waste time, to not follow too closely, and to communicate with the leader.

STOP!

EDDY OUT!

Hand signs

You are on wild water; steep, roaring, and loud, right? As a consequence, verbal communication is only possible when you're close together. Otherwise you'll need to communicate with hand signals. The following are basic essentials which will allow you to guide a paddler or warn him of dangers. The signals can be freely combined, but note:
less is more; keep it simple so as not to confuse the others!

> **Tip**

Regardless of how clear your signals are, the Golden Rule is:
> Always point at the recommended line or route, never at the obstacle!
> Always give other paddlers enough space for spontaneous maneuvers!

LEFT!

BOOF!

WARNING ROCK!

DOWN THE MIDDLE!

TREE!

TOWARDS ME!

UNRUNNABLE!

SCOUT!

GIVE IT ALL YOU'VE GOT!

Tactical maneuvers

Eddy turns with a bow rudder and forward stroke combination

Above a drop you normally take the last eddy to look over the ledge, and as a consequence you might not have enough space to accelerate your boat for a safe run. This is where you need the combination of a draw and forward stroke.

Exit the eddy with a strong forward momentum and at a right angle to the eddy line. As soon as your bow crosses the eddy line, edge your boat and place your bow rudder far downstream, and cross the eddy line into main current. Throw your upper body well downstream! Turn your boat around the paddle and bring your weight back over the boat. As soon as your bow rudder reaches the level of your feet, the pressure on the paddle decreases (this means your boat is now as fast as the current). To achieve maximum acceleration of your boat, do a steep, strong forward stroke. This stroke combination also works if you want to eddy out.

Throw your upper body courageously downstream – place your bow rudder in the main current – as soon as the pressure on your paddle decreases, transfer into a forward stroke

> **Tip**

> – The face of the paddle must point upstream!
> – Accelerate hard towards the eddy line and leave out the sweep stroke on the downriver side.
> – Dig your paddle into the main current before you leave the eddy.
> – Do your draw stroke in the main current and not in the turbulence of the eddy line.
> – The draw stroke will only work if you are leaning well into the turn– only then can you dig the paddle vertically into the water and get the maximum pull.
> – Always adjust the position of your blade to achieve maximum pressure.

The back ferry

On technical white water, you often approach an obstructed section slowly, and feel your way towards it doing backstrokes.
In doing so you can win time needed to find a line. If you suddenly find that a passage is unboatable or too obstructed, you often don't have the space or the time to turn your boat around by 180°, so it's time for a back ferry – the emergency brake and last chance of correction for brave hearted white water warriors. The backward ferry is not a new technique, it is simply a reversed forward ferry. Nonetheless you should master it before you have to apply it in case of emergency.

Back ferry in the Lofer gorge, Austria

Tactical eddy turns

Doing eddy turns in a cataract can be a tactical maneuver. A tactical eddy enables you to:
– Check the further course of the cataract.
– Cross the river with the help of a midstream eddy.
– Hit your desired line safely.
– Reach the eddy you are aiming for with an additional eddy turn (Principle: if you want to go left, you have to come from the right).

A good tactical line, including an extra loop, in the "S" of the Lofer gorge

... The most popular way to deal with certain experiences?

Head work

Digesting experiences

White water paddling is an inherently dangerous sport. You cannot avoid swimming from time to time and you are not safe from accidents or injuries.

Serious accidents traumatize you and can leave you afraid of experiencing something comparable again. But even smaller accidents remain stored subconsciously. In the course of time these traumas can accumulate to a critical mass and then fear overwhelms the fun of paddling.

Try to digest every accident – mental injuries only get cured if you find rational reasons for accidents, such as mistakes, technical deficits, or ignorance.

You can avoid or work on these potential causes in the future, and will thus reduce the risk of making the same mistake twice. If you also learn from the mistakes of others, you greatly speed your learning, profiting from their experience as well. If you cannot explain the accident rationally, you have probably overshot your mental stress limits. Try to learn and accept your emotional limits.

The common "no brain no pain", or "blind is bliss" approach of dicing with destiny does not bring you any further, it only leads you to your next borderline experience.

> Tip

> "Also learn from the mistakes of others - who knows whether you would survive making the same one."
> Miles Dasher, B.A.S.E Jumper

Tricks

Rely on your eskimo roll

Fear-free learning is the best learning. The biggest problem for a novice might be the fear of capsizing. Therefore it is very important to automate your roll by practicing it, over and over again. Capsize in turbulent waves, capsize in technical sections, capsize in pools – technique and routine come only from repetition. Practice makes perfect!

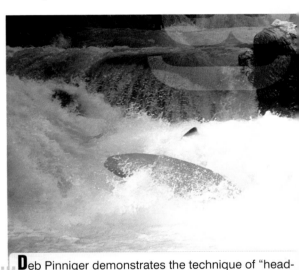

Deb Pinniger demonstrates the technique of "head-ruddering" . Whitcombe river, New Zealand

Playboating and surfing

Playboating is the ultimate training for white water paddlers. There is no better way to improve your technique and boat control than surfing waves, splatting rocks or riding holes. Playboating is also one of the best roll training grounds you can get – nowhere else on a river will you capsize more often than riding a hole. Check out the book "Rodeo Boating" for more details.

Ingrid Schlott surfin' the Salzach river near Kuchl, Austria

Clear message on the Travo river, Corsica

3x3 Method – avoiding accidents on whitewater

"As long as we cannot preclude uncertainty with scientific methods, we must make a science of dealing with uncertainty ". (Werner Munter)

Why are so many people nervous before they paddle a new river?
It is their fear of the unknown.

Werner Munter, from the Institute for Snow and Avalanche Research in Davos, Switzerland, is familiar with this nervousness. He knows that you must face many unknowns during an adventure, nevertheless he sees the possibility of limiting the variables in such a way as to make a ski tour a calculated risk – as paradoxical as this may sound.

When in 1997 Munter published his book "3x3 Avalanches – decision in critical situations", a loud murmur could be heard in the world of alpinism. Until that time avalanche research had been a physical science which did not consider the "human factor" as a cause for skier avalanches. Munter was the first to bring people into this calculation, and he included factors such as inaccurate self assessment, group pressure and personal competence in the equation for decisions on the mountain.

Since a kayak trip can be likened to a ski tour in many respects, Munter's catalogue of questions lends itself well to planning a day of paddling. This checklist is as well suited to beginners as to experts – it ensures that all relevant issues are considered, so that informed decisions are made.

It enables beginners to structure the complex world of an alpine river landscape rationally, and thus to understand the correlation between the various elements.

The 3x3 method uses 3 criteria, including environmental and human factors, which are examined according to 3 filters.

The 3 criteria

- The **conditions**, which include the weather, the geography and the geology of a region.

- The **character of a river**, the riverbed and the difficulties.

- **Man**, characterized by his skills and abilities, his actions and his equipment.

The 3 Filters

- The **planning of the trip** at home.

- The **selection of a run**.

- The **decision at the cataract**.

In the following, the correlations are explained. They constitute the base of information which is relevant for a decision in any phase of the trip.

First filter: the planning of the trip

In the planning stage you consider possibilities, and choose an appropriate goal.

 Planning of the trip / conditions

- River guide books
- Is there any first hand information?
- Region
- Catchment area
- Weather forecast
- Snow base
- Expected water levels
- Relief
- Rock

If you are planning a trip there are many relevant aspects to consider. To be able to assess the expected water levels, you should have information about the height of the catchment area of the rivers, the current snow base and the weather forecast. Important factors are also temperature and the amount of rain during the last days. For instance, snow melt starts only when the temperature in higher regions, also at night, rises well above 0° C.

The risk of rock and snow avalanches or tree jams also differs greatly from one region to the other, whereas the rivers in one region may all share a very similar character. On Corsica for example, it is more likely to find steep rivers with low volume, whereas in the Oetztal, you are more likely to encounter big volume during the summer.

 Planning of the trip / river character

- River guide books/ photos/ personal knowledge
- V-Valley/ box canyon/ open riverbed
- High volume or steep
- Character of the river bed

Information about a river's character can mostly be found in guide books or photos, and you choose your equipment e.g. boat, a split paddle and elbow pads, accordingly.

 Planning of the trip / man

- Who is on the trip?
- Physical/ mental condition
- Equipment
- Experience/ skills
- Preferences

Especially in the planning phase it is important to set goals at a realistic level – they must be customized to the abilities of the group. Check with your fellow paddlers about their preferences, their experience and their equipment.

Second filter: selecting a run

When selecting a run it is necessary to check the expectations of the group and to collect up-to-date information at the river.

 Selecting a run / conditions

- Weather
- Water level/ gauge level
- Bank access, box canyon
- Snow or rock avalanches, storms, high flow, tree jams, construction sites

Once you have reached the river, check the weather and all the other natural conditions. These factors could include rain, thunderstorms, or heat which cause a river to rise within hours. You must also check for remaining snow and rock avalanches, storms, tree jams, flood or a construction site in the gorge which can make a rapid a highly dangerous trap.

 Selecting a run / river character

- Are my expectations of the river's character and the conditions of the bank accurate?
- Have I observed unexpected dangers in the river such as sharp rocks, siphons or a lack of eddies?
- Does the river have pools or is it a full-on motorway?
- Is the river's difficulty accurately graded?
- Is it possible to abandon the run at any time?

When you have reached the river, compare the details in the guide book with the river's actual character. Running or driving along the river gives you a fairly quick and precise picture of the prevailing conditions. But beware, the most difficult passages are usually very hard to scout, since they are mostly hidden in deep and inaccessible gorges. So be prepared to spend time scouting, especially on difficult rivers.

 Selecting a run / man

- Are the skills, experience and gear suited to the given conditions?
- Do we have a fitting time schedule?
- Who is coming along?
- Who else is on the river?

Once you have gathered as much objective information as possible, and have measured it against your skills and gear, there is nothing left to hold you back…

Third filter: at the cataract

At the cataract you make your final decision about running a rapid.

 Cataract / conditions

- Weather
- Temperature
- Falling rocks
- Water level

You also have to constantly check peripheral factors. For example, is a thunderstorm building or is it too cold to perform adequately?

 Cataract / character of the river

- Bank
- Consequences
- What awaits us downstream?

The river's character will always influence strategic decisions. Is the bank accessible in the case of a rescue or a portage? What are the consequences if I miss the line and capsize? What is the situation like downstream?

 Cataract / man

- Check your schedule
- Condition: exhaustion, mood, motivation, injury
- Possibilities for a rescue

Even an expert paddler can be knocked out by exhaustion or a bad mood – always make your decisions based on the individual condition of your fellow paddlers.

At this point the 3x3 method's chain of decisions ends, and the classical tactics of running a rapid begin. It's all in your hands now!

Summary

The 3x3 method for paddlers is a new concept which was first adapted for kayaking by Christoph Mayer of Freiburg/ Germany. For newcomers it can be a brilliant means of orientation in an alpine river landscape. With time it will be reviewed, discussed and improved, so if you have any comments or ideas about it, please do not hesitate to contact the publisher of this book.

○ conditions	→	○ character	→	○ man

Planning a trip

conditions
- River guide books
- Is there any first hand information?
- Region
- Catchment area
- Weather forecast
- Snow base
- Expected water levels
- Relief
- Rock

character
- River guides/ photos/ personal knowledge
- V-Valley/ box canyon/ open riverbed
- High volume or steep
- Character of the river bed

man
- Who is on the trip?
- Physical/ mental condition
- Equipment
- Experience/ skills
- Preferences

selecting a run

conditions
- Weather
- Water level
- Bank access, box canyon
- Snow or rock avalanches
- storms
- high flow
- tree jams, construction sites

character
- Are my expectations of the river's character and the conditions of the bank accurate?
- Have I observed unexpected dangers in the river such as sharp rocks, siphons or a lack of eddies?
- Does the river have pools or is it more of a motorway?
- Is the river's difficulty accurately graded?
- Is it possible to abandon the run at any time?

man
- Are the skills, experience and gear suited to the given conditions?
- Do we have an appropriate schedule?
- Who is coming along?
- Who else is on the river?

Cataract

conditions
- Weather
- Temperature
- Falling rocks
- Water level

character
- Bank
- Consequences
- What awaits us downstream?

man
- Check your schedule
- Shape: exhaustion, mood, motivation, injury
- Possibilities for a rescue

Calculating risks and overcoming personal challenges

Extreme white water, class 4-5

The majority of skiers in the Alps ski blue or red runs, and only a few rip down the diamond runs, or dare a high alpine glacier run. Paddling is similar – you meet most paddlers on class 2 - 3 rivers.

Breathtaking unportageable drop on the Averser Rhein, Switzerland

White water paddling up to class 3 is a leisure activity, but beyond class 4 it is an extreme sport. There are few truly "extreme" kayakers who get their paddling kicks from running highly dangerous, super sick lines or rivers.

If you are stuck in a deep gorge or canyon, you are on your own, and are entirely responsible for your actions. Paddling extreme white water not only requires brilliant paddling skills and good equipment, but also a knowledge of mountain rescue, first aid and rock climbing. Not to mention good overall physical shape. This is an alpine sport which demands that you combine awareness and skilled handling of peripheral conditions, the river and people and their traits.
A successful run rewards your patience and determination with a flood of endorphins, and a seldom felt, deep sense of satisfaction.

Class 4 – very difficult

Line of sight: passages normally obstructed and have to be scouted.
Water: big wave trains, strong holes, whirlpools, boils and pillows.
Riverbed: offset rocks in the current, higher drops with back tows.

Class 5 – extremely difficult

Line of sight: scouting essential
Water: extreme wave trains, extreme holes, whirlpools, boils and pillows
Riverbed: very tight and technical, high drops with difficult approaches and exits

A few words about class 6

Class 6 represents the absolute limit of what can be paddled, and demands spectacular stunts which are only possible at certain water levels. It takes many years of paddling at an extreme level before you are able to assess and run such rapids. No-one should ever encourage anyone else to paddle grade six. Rivers and rapids of this difficulty are beyond objective judgment, and the decision to paddle them can carry grave consequences. Such a decision must be made personally, without pressure from peers or thoughts of heroism.

class 4 Sorba, Italy

class 5 Lucifer's slide, Verzasca, Italy

class 6 Schorschi Schauf on the Rhinefall in Schaffhausen, Switzerland

White water anatomy

Canyons and gorges

Extreme white water always has a steep gradient, and steep, difficult rivers run in narrow gorges and canyons. Before we go deeper into the anatomical features of white water, we need to discuss the characteristics of such valleys.

The river is the deepest point of a valley, and everything that slides down from the valley walls ends up in the river. This means that you face a high risk of falling rocks, especially during heavy rain fall. Trees which end up in the riverbed after storms, logging work or avalanches can form perilous tree jams.

For a paddler, a canyon is characterized by its bank line. If there is no access to the bank and portaging is impossible, you are facing a must-run rapid. Check such a passage previous to your run – is it possible, are there any obstacles or trees? Normally such passages get mentioned in river guide books.
Since it is usually difficult to climb out of a gorge, it is essential to start early enough to leave time for such an escape if necessary. Even a minor accident can cost you a few hours time. Your equipment must also be suited to the conditions in a gorge – always carry a first-aid kit and a spare paddle.

In gorges you will probably have one of the most intense experiences of white water. The damp, cold atmosphere and the roar of the river in a gorge takes you into a world accessible to paddlers only. The tighter the walls of the gorge get, the more likely there is only one way out – down the river. Be prepared or stay away!

Grand Canyon of the Stikine River, Canada

Unportageable rapid "Wassons Hole",
Stikine, Canada

Weir-like waterfall,
Verzasca, Switzerland

so-called V-wave is formed. If a diagonal line "feeds" into a diagonal hole or a wave, it is called the shoulder.

Diagonals from the right

Diagonals

Waves, breaking waves or holes which run diagonally to the main current are called diagonals. They form a strong cross current in the direction of their course and can either help a paddler to cross from one side to another, or can throw him seriously off line. When two diagonals meet from opposite directions, a

Drops and waterfalls

Waterfalls are the most beautiful and spectacular phenomena in white water – a clean, high waterfall is the highlight of any river trip. There are countless forms of waterfalls, but two basic differences in form are identified – weir or jet like. The running of a waterfall is split into the approach, the edge, the fall and landing.

A potential route is normally oriented towards the landing. The ideal situation is a deep pool in which the water is well aerated, thus forming a soft landing.

If the pool has a strong back tow, a run is only possible for low drops.
At higher drops, you lose your forward momentum during the free fall, and the pool's back tow will most likely hold you.

The edge of the fall is another deciding point, and ideally should be abrupt to better enable a boof. A rounded and rolling edge is ideal for the so-called drift wood technique.

The currents of the approach and the ledge give a waterfall its individual form. The approach must enable you to reach the desired take-off point of the ledge.

If the jet is twisted by a cushion, or if two currents cross from different directions, choose the top current.

Jet waterfall on the Store Ula, Norway

Slide on the Egua, Italy

Slides

A granite slide covered with crystal clear water is an experience for both the paddler and the observer. Nowhere else can you experience acceleration and weightless gliding as intensely as on a steep slide.

After entering a steep slide, your trajectory along the fall line is predetermined, and the only thing you can do is keep the boat straight. On slides you have to be especially careful of the current's slope and drift. Plan your approach so that you have only to follow the fall line.

The slope pushes the main current to the right, seen from downstream. South fork of the Yuba River, California, USA

Side slope and drift

The gradient of the river across the current is called side slope. Such a "hanging" riverbed can often only be recognized from downstream. Even in a straight river section the current pulls in the direction of the deeper "hanging" bank, and paddling an "uphill line" becomes difficult.

Every river bend has a drift towards the outside of the turn, because the inertia of the mass pushes the water in this direction. It is difficult to paddle against this drift, and if this is made stronger by a side slope, it very soon becomes impossible to paddle your boat to the inside of a turn. On the other hand, if you have a slope to the inside of a bend, it can counteract the drift.

Undercuts and siphons

Both slope and drift are decisive factors for hitting a line, which until now have been paid little attention in kayak training. If the line follows the drift or the slope of the river, nothing can really go wrong. But woe unto those who did not take them into account and have to work against them!

Slope and drift are considered not only in relation to the whole riverbed, but also to passages and in particular sections of the river.

Undercuts and siphons are the killers in white water, and most fatal accidents on rivers happen around them. Even siphons that would be wide enough to fit a swimming body through, are mostly obstructed with driftwood, forming an impenetrable barrier. Always check for undercut walls and rocks if you are scouting or planning your line. Try to give them a wide berth.

If, despite all caution, you find yourself drifting towards an undercut, you must avoid capsiz-ing. Only if you lean towards the undercut obstacle early enough you can keep your boat away from the obstacle and push yourself off from it.

The drift is so strong that a gigantic pillow is formed right on the edge of the drop. South Yuba, California

Current flowing sideways under an overhanging rock. Soca, Slovenia

A log jam in a siphon. Lofer gorge, Austria

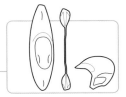

Body check

If you are trying to test your personal limits you need to make sure that all your senses are working at a hundred percent – anything less is irresponsible. Even a cold, a hangover or personal problems can dull your awareness so that you are not able to perform fully. When you want to push the envelope, what counts is the so-called form on the day. The most difficult thing can be admitting to yourself that you are having a bad day.

Physical fitness and the ability to concentrate are closely related. If you are physically exhausted, you lose your concentration pretty quickly. So, work on your condition and your endurance in preparation for serious challenges.

Antique depiction of youthful high spirits and well trained bodies

117

Preparatory work

Every relaxed day on a river should be seen as practice for tougher duties on a more difficult river. Never enter a critical situation unprepared, a difficult project should be worked on months in advance. Good physical shape, familiarity with difficult rivers, practice of technical skills and a test of your equipment all belong to the preparation, and these give you the required mental strength for spectacular and difficult runs.

Safety equipment

On serious white water you must make no compromise with your gear – when it comes to safety, the best gear is the right gear. Every boat has to have a throw bag with two carabiners and pulleys. Always wear a knife and a cowtail, and a whistle can simplify communication.

If you are heading for deep gorges and canyons, your group should carry at least one spare split paddle. A tubular webbing sling (120 cm) can be a very helpful device when it comes to rescue. Use it as a seat harness, along with an abseiling eight and an HMS-carabiner on alpine adventures. Other items you must carry with you if you are out in the bush and away from civilization is a lighter, a rescue blanket and a first-aid kit. About a meter of duct tape, wrapped around your shaft, helps you with minor repairs.

Tubular webbing as a seat harness

> Tip

> If you can't duct it, chuck it.

Handles for rescue

A roomy cockpit for a safe emergency exit

The right boat

for extreme rivers has many safety features concerning its performance and its passive safety.

White water boats for steep, low volume creeks are short (220-245 cm), have a lot of rocker and high volume ends. These are easy to boof, are virtually pin-proof, and resurface quickly. Boats for big water are longer (245-280 cm), have less rocker and are faster. Stern and bow have less volume, are therefore better suited to breaking through waves and holes, and track better in pushy cataracts.
The volume of a white water boat must suit your body weight (240-300 liters and upwards). Extra volume literally keeps the head up. The type of boat you choose depends on your preferences in white water and paddling region.

There is no room for compromise when it comes to the fittings of your white water weapon. The safety handles have to be rock solid – stiff metal bars are great for attaching carabiners, but are definitely not suited for longer portages, so simply add some extra loops out of tubular webbing. The cockpit rim has to be large enough for a safe exit in case of emergency, and it should be cut deep enough to hold the spray skirt even under extreme conditions. The foot room needs to

be spacious enough that you can sit in your boat with sturdy paddling shoes, and the full plate footrest must be robust. A safe boat has roto-molded PE-parts for the seat and the center block, which must be attached to the hull with screws. Only then can a boat hold its shape in a pin situation after the spray skirt has been opened to enable an exit. The center block should have a step – this is the one thing that will enable you to exit the boat if you are pinned vertically. And don't forget the air bags!

Split paddle

In exposed gorges or on remote trips, you should carry a spare paddle. Make sure that it can be switched for a "lefty"!

The spare split paddle is stored in the stern

In springtime the summits of Graubuenden still shine white. Averser Rhine, Switzerland

Technique

The good line, the dry line

"A fluent, controlled and predictable run is the aim of all techniques and tactics in white water."

It looks like child's play when experts run a class 5 cataract. They paddle raging torrents and don't even get their hair wet. What is their secret? Why does a leisure paddler get thrown around, while the pros glide smoothly and graciously through the water? The secret is called "the dry line".

The dry line has its origins in open canoe paddling, and aims for a flowing and direct line through a current, resulting in a dry run without taking on water. For an open canoe this is a technique of pure survival on big water, since it begins to lose its navigability as soon as it takes on water. A kayak with a spray skirt is not as affected by waves and breakers, even though they definitely influence your performance. When you get swamped by a wave you lose speed and maneuverability, and need a lot more energy to stay on line.
With the following tricks you will keep your boat on the surface, and will glide over anything that would stop you or throw you off your line.

Besides waves and holes there are so-called half-eddies which you should also master.

Waves and holes

One way to cross waves and holes and stay dry is to paddle over their shoulders, where they are least steep. Or if possible circumnavigate them altogether, even if this means leaving your line.

If you have to cross a wave or a hole in its mid section, approach it with a slightly angled boat and lift it onto the foam pile with a strong sweep stroke on the upstream side. Edge the boat upstream, lift your bow and keep paddling.

This technique is especially well suited for small waves and holes, and requires precise timing. However, if the wave or hole is too big it can easily lead to a back flip. Make sure that you have enough speed. Later on we will discuss how to manage big waves and holes, in which you will find no such thing as a dry line...

With a stroke in the falling green water, lift your bow onto the foam pile

Half eddies

In a cataract you will often find small midstream eddies or slower currents. These are caused by a rock beneath the surface. To cross such a half eddy, you have to approach it at a steep angle from upstream. As soon as you cross the eddy line, edge your boat upstream and let the slow water flow underneath your boat. Support your forward momentum with a strong sweep stroke on the upstream side and finish with a rudder stroke on the same side. Edge your boat downstream as you reach the main current on the other side of the half eddy, and let the fast moving water pass underneath. The edge change is as for eddy turns.

Glide through a half eddy behind a hole with strong upstream sweep stroke

Boofing

When you boof, you jump the drop and land flat in the pool without submerging.

The boof technique helps you to hold a dry line, even on big drops. It makes the impossible possible, and boosts your performance no end. Without a perfect boofing technique you will be forever stuck on class 3 rivers. A solid boof sorts the 'boys from the men', and is to the advanced boater what the Eskimo roll is to the novice.

As you approach the edge of the drop, prepare for the last, decisive stroke and the "flight" early enough. Sit on both buttocks with a slight forward lean – get your weight off the backrest! As soon as the edge comes into reach, your stroking hand should already be in the forward position. Check your paddle blade and plant the last stroke right behind the edge into the falling water. Pull hard on your forward stroke, keep your arms long, rotate your upper body sideways and push your hip forward, thus shooting your center of gravity across the ledge. Now pull your knees up with the help of your belly muscles before the boat tilts down.

In short boats this forward momentum is sufficient to push your stern across the ledge and to keep the boat horizontal while in the air. Get into a forward lean combat position right after the stroke, because this is best for landing a boof. With a slight forward lean and a low paddle position, you can absorb the impact, keep your balance, and be ready to paddle on.

If you are doing extremely high boofs, or landing on green water, you face a high risk of injury. The impact can be so hard that your vertebrae can get compressed or even break. Nose fractures on the rim of the cockpit are also not uncommon. So if you are expecting a hard landing, you should choose the so-called drift wood technique. If you have to boof because the pool is not deep enough or there is a back tow, await the impact in an extreme forward lean, hold your paddle parallel to the boat, and protect your face with your front arm.

Aim for the edge – place your last stroke right behind it and remain in a forward lean

Flatter drops have to be boofed late, with the last stroke shortly before you hit the pool

> **Tip**

> Remain seated on both buttocks during the take off – this way you keep your balance even on a big drop.

> Check where you place your last stroke and keep an eye on your active blade!

> Take your time planning the approach!

Crossing diagonals

Crossing a strong diagonal without being offset requires a precise approach. The boat needs maximum forward speed at a right angle to the diagonal current, meaning that it has to be accelerated across the main current.

Again: if you are heading left, you have to come from the right.

If you want to break through a diagonal running from the right to the middle of the river, the best approach is to come from the left or at least from the center of the river. This gives you room to accelerate. You may intentionally paddle to the left of the river center, to then be able to build up speed heading back to the right!

Edge the boat downstream right in front of the diagonal current and push it onto the foam pile with a strong downstream sweep stroke. Immediately dig the paddle upstream into the backside of the diagonal and pull the boat out.

> **Tip**

> If you are heading right, you have to come from the left!

With the right speed and angle of approach, a little edging downriver and a strong downriver sweep stroke, you can break through almost any diagonal

Riding diagonals

It is a lot easier if the diagonal is running in your direction of travel, because you simply have to "get on". You ride the diagonal just like a hole or a pillow, with your boat aligned parallel to it. Do a rudder stroke to then point the boat downstream once more.

The less foam the diagonal has, the less it will hold you and allow you to surf across it. The weaker the diagonal is, the further you should point your bow upstream, as with a ferry glide, or you may even go into a front surf to cross it.

If you approach parallel, you'll follow the diagonal

Down time

Even though you normally try to stay on the surface, there are situations in which you want to get some down time. Diving through a breaking wave or diving deep into the green-room of a waterfall allows you to enter the heart of a river. Entering this other dimension is as scary as it is fascinating, and nowhere else you can feel the river's might and power so intensely.

Duck and cover as an exercise...

Duck and cover

A head high breaking wave offers you no other choice than to dive under it, and this move is called "duck and cover". For this you duck your upper body forward in order to offer the foam pile as small a target as possible – not forgetting to get up enough speed first! Cover stands for covering the spray skirt with your upper body while you break through the wave. It is best to take your paddle as far forward as possible and as you break through dig your front hand into the green water and pull into a strong forward stroke.

Regardless of how strong the breaking wave might be, you remain in this forward position, and if you capsize you are ready to roll right away.

...and the real thing. Stikine river, Canada

Meltdowns

Waterfalls and slides where you want to go for down time, or a meltdown, are pretty rare. It is usually best to glide down passively (at the same speed as the water) in a combat position, with a good forward lean, and a good breath hold.
However, be aware that this can in some cases cause you to pop back out again, and not make it through the back tow.

Drift wood technique

The higher the waterfall gets and the less aerated the pool is, the more you want to plug into the pool with an almost vertical boat angle, to ease the deceleration on impact. As you approach, accelerate the boat to the speed of the current and let yourself drift towards the edge, like a tree being carried in the current. Cross the edge at a point where it is rounded and gentle.

Here it is recommendable to decelerate smoothly. Flemming Schmidt on the Store Ula, Norway

Short meltdown on the Ardezer gorge of the Inn River, Switzerland

Safety

Active and passive safety

Awareness for safety is your life insurance in extreme white water. Accidents beyond class 4 often have serious consequences. This chapter deals with dangers in extreme white water, and offers some options for worst case scenarios.

The most decisive aspect of safety remains active safety – your paddling skills. Far too often groups can be seen on the bank of a class 5 river, establishing the wildest safety set ups – probably because they will most likely need them! Hardly anyone ever figures out that the river is simply too difficult if they require so much passive safety.

There are certainly situations in which securing is obligatory, but you should never rely on it. Running a rapid and counting on being rescued is simply irresponsible, above all with regard to the rescuers – they often face an even higher risk than you do!

There are two famous cases in which paddlers who were trying to help their buddies drowned; Mike Jones who did the first run of the Dudh Kosi, starting at the Everest base camp, and Francois Cirotteau, a famous french creek paddler in the nineties.

Group dynamics and self-reflection

An accident often results from a so-called "risky shift" effect. This effect rests on the theory that a risky decision is normally followed by an even riskier decision, and this leads to a fatal chain of events which ultimately results in a serious accident. Such a process often emerges in groups where there is a sense of competition among the members. This supports what psychologist Bernhard Streicher sees as two equally important causes of wrong decisions:

1. The lack of competence in collecting and evaluating important information.
2. Psychological processes and processes related to group dynamics.

I don't wish to condemn risky behavior – as long as nobody else is endangered – but would like to differentiate between conscious and inadvertent risk taking. Conscious risk taking is one of the greatest expressions of freedom we have in paddling. Inadvertent risky behavior is a different matter altogether, because a little thinking can avoid so much trouble and injury.

Pins

If a kayak gets stuck against a rock or between two rocks in the current, we call it a pin. If the boat is stuck vertically we call it a vertical pin. Both pins are, next to swimming, the most critical situations possible on a river trip. Especially if the paddler is caught under water and cannot breathe – red alert!

Pin on the Sorba, Italy

Boat pinned sideways against two rocks

Self rescue

With many pins, quick-witted action helps best. The worst disasters can often be avoided in the last second. Shaking or rocking the boat hard or pushing with the paddle is often enough to set you free. If the situation is already hopeless or so delicate that you do not want to risk worsening it, the only option left is the emergency exit.

The discussion about kayak cockpits is almost as old as paddling itself. How big can a cockpit be to allow a safe exit, but still hold the spray skirt well enough? The answer is pretty simple: as big as necessary, as small as possible. The individual personal variables are height, length of your legs and the diameter of your thighs. In a safe cockpit, fitted with thigh braces, you should be able to take both knees out at a time, while remaining seated. This means that you will be able to exit the boat with water pressure on your back. For years this means of exiting has been valued as the safest in the event of a pin. And it is surely the best technique for avoiding a fatal "knee-hanger" in the boat. For a vertical pin this technique has only one disadvantage – you can fall out of the boat head first, probably landing on the rock which has trapped you and your boat. Furthermore, it is possible that your lower leg get stuck in the cockpit.

A second technique is suited especially for a vertical pin situation, or if you are confronted with water pressure from behind. In this case you use the center block as a step for the first leg and your cockpit rim for the second.

A knee-hanger

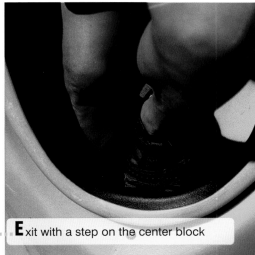

Exit with a step on the center block

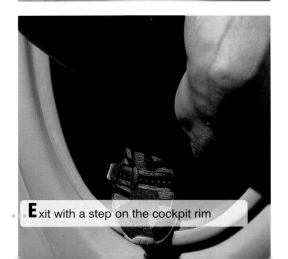

Exit with a step on the cockpit rim

Exit with both legs

Salvaging a boat

Even in the case of a harmless "swim", the abandoned boat can get stuck and have to be salvaged.

The general rule for this situation is:

Fix a rope to the nearest handle of the boat, or to the one that is pointing upstream, and pull it out in the upstream direction. For this you can use pulleys and tubular webbing in order to optimize the direction of pull and achieve mechanical advantage.

If the boat is stuck in the middle of the river and has to be reached by swimming, it is best to secure the rescuer with a rope.

Tricks:

There are a bunch of tricks to help you in particular situations.

- If a boat is stuck right behind a narrow slot, jam another boat upstream across the slot to reduce the water pressure.
- If a boat is jammed in front of a rock, fix the rope tightly to a tree and pull the tight rope with a jerk and your whole weight.
- You can easily release a vertically pinned boat if you are able to lift its stern above the water line.
- Fix a carabiner to a paddle blade with some duct tape to bridge the distance to the boat. (Always bring at least a meter of duct tape wrapped around your shaft)

The best way to release a vertical pin is to pull upstream

Drift wood allows you to quickly get an anchor point on the bank

You can sometimes free the boat yourself with a perpendicular pull on a rope tied tightly tightened between the boat and an anchor point

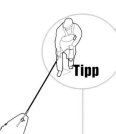

Tipp

> If somebody is pinned, your first job is to ensure he's able to breathe!

> The best way to pull a boat out of a vertical pin is to pull against the direction in which it got caught.

> When exiting a boat after a pin it can be very helpful to have a throw bag to hold on to.

Tactics and maneuvers

Paddling in big water

We already know that following the highest waves normally means the best line. If the waves are extremely high, let yourself drift towards them slightly sideways. This means less water in your face and a better look downriver.

Big volume rivers run fast and require paddling with good foresight. Approach river bends on the outside to get an overview. If you cannot find your line right away, but still don't think that you need to scout, head for the inside of the curve to have all possible alternatives at hand.

A lot of rivers in the Alps are just one long cataract. Flying down class 4 rapids for kilometers without eddies is a special thrill. Especially when these rivers are running at high flows, it can be impossible to stop in front of every

Scouting from the top of a wave...

cataract. Indeed, by exiting you are often moving away from the optimal line, bringing yourself into a tactically bad position.

New Zealands west coast offers whitewater at its best

...or from the last eddy

Jens Klatt using the limiting rock for a boof. Saalach river, Austria

Paddling technical rivers and steep creeks

Large numbers of big rocks slow the river's current and form eddies. In technical white water you can scout quite a lot from the boat and "hop" from one eddy to the other.

If you are on a difficult river, you always have to be aware of the possibility of a key move or a portage right behind the next rock. That's why you should head for tactical eddies only if you are 100% sure of being able to catch them. Never take your eye off the bank – if your last eddy does not allow you to get back or to portage, you are one eddy too far...

Paddling upstream

Every slalom paddler knows the story of paddling upstream – over and over again your coach chases you through the same combination of gates. After each run you have to paddle back up, from one eddy to the next.

Nevertheless, there is no better way to practice edging, stroke technique and eddy turns than this simple exercise. If you are well praticed in paddling upstream, you will be able to judge your abilities for tricky ferries and eddies much more accurately.

The line for a boof

A waterfall can be divided into four different sections: the approach, the edge, the fall and the pool. All four sections are of equal importance for the paddler's line over the waterfall.

The steeper the water is falling, the easier it is to initiate a boof. Once you have found the steepest point of the waterfall, it is time to answer a few more questions:
Is there enough water flowing over the edge at the steepest point? Which side can you dig the paddle in for the boof stroke?

Can you reach this point quickly from upstream? Where is your landing after the boof?

Are there little boof aids, like a natural launch pad or a wave that you can use?

In so-called U-shaped falls, the steepest point can mostly be found in the middle, where the back tow is also strongest. If the back tow is an issue, you should choose your line according to the flowing water below the drop, and disregard the steepest point. The best approach for running a back tow is to hit the edge at its most downstream point.

Often you can boof falls to the right or left hand side in order to avoid the back tow.

Once you have found your spot on the edge, you have to decide which side you are going to place the boof stroke. If you are boofing to the right or to the left, you simply place the stroke on the opposite side. Boofing in the center is a little more difficult, so you have to review your approach: if you are approaching in an arc, you will place your last stroke on the inside of the turn. If you are approaching the fall in a straight line, you simply place your stroke where you have the deepest water.

Surfing back tows

Everybody gets a beating some time. You will also screw up a line or underestimate a back tow and get stuck.
Don't give up right away! As long as you are still sitting upright you have a chance of escaping. Even after a lengthy cycle in the "washing machine" you often come back into an upright position, away from the falling water – that's your chance!
Keep fighting, but not to your last breath – you will need it if you have to exit the boat and swim or dive out of the back tow!

Battle with the back tow on the Egua, Italy

Moves and anchor points

A situation in a car could look like this: you are looking far ahead because you do not want miss the next exit, but you also see the immediate surroundings – the exit of a yard with a playing kid, or the rock right ahead of you in your lane.

This is how you build up a line through a cataract. First you choose the main line, then split it up into the different moves (for example: hit the eddy behind this rock, or boof that drop) and attribute each with a certain level of difficulty. The more difficult the move is, the greater the detail required to plan it. This can go as far as analyzing the smallest currents, or planning strokes to the centimeter.

Every move has a goal. These goals are not only important for visualizing your line, but also as psychological anchor points. If you reach your goal in a cataract with a number of moves, you have already partly won the battle, and are on the road to victory and glory!

"**E**yes shut tight and go" is definitely not the way to face your fears

Head work

Management of fear

The flow

Somewhere between panic and boredom there is a mood which is simply euphoric. Sports scientists and psychologists call it "the flow".

This is a state of mind of total concentration and alertness – you are working at 100%, using all your mental and physical capacities. In this particular state of mind you experience yourself, the river and your environment deeply, and generate powerful positive memories.

He who paddles white water has a story to tell: "...I was paddling the Loisach once, at high flow...." This was obviously a flow experience!

A flow experience is generated if you succeed in pushing your limits to the right degree. Learn to face, to analyze and to categorize your fears!

Internal communication

Fear and white water go hand in hand. Fear inspires respect for a river, and is a natural safety mechanism. Good internal communication is a prerequisite for a serious battle with your fear.

Look at the river and try to find the roots of your fear. Is it a hole, an undercut, or are you scared of screwing up the roll? Once you can identify the source of your fear, you can work on it and eliminate it, whatever the cause. The best paddlers are said to be absolutely fearless, but despite a few exceptions, this is in fact not the case. The difference is that they have good fear management, and work constantly on their weak points. Fear of technical failure can be fought in the long term.

If you are not already confronted with a decision situation in a cataract, the best thing to do is to scout your intended run over and over again. Information alone is often enough to eliminate the large part of personal fears. If you have collected all the possible information, found a line, excluded technical failure and still feel scared, then the most delicate point of overcoming fear is yet to come.

Alarming and paralyzing fear

Is your fear within the physiological "green" range and is it not blocking you, or is it already close to panic? It is a fine line. As long as your fear does not block you, the run will be a flow experience and normally nothing will go wrong, because your whole body is in an alert state. If you are in the "red" range, you mostly screw your run up, because fear paralyzes. Even if you make it through you can't really rejoice – it would have been better to portage.

It is very difficult to differentiate between the green and the red range – to free yourself from group constraints and thoughts of heroism. Only once you find yourself and your inner voice are you able to make the right decisions in a borderline situation. With some experience you will start to feel motivation in the green range and paralysis in the red.

Form on the day/ the seventh sense

For good fear management your form on the day is of great importance. Listen to your body, your inner voice, the so-called seventh sense, which every human being has. It is as important as your rational reasons for being afraid, since about 80% of our perception is based on subconscious phenomena, and only 20% based on conscious knowledge.

The inner pre-run

Close your eyes and try to visualize your intended run as seen from the boat. Regard all points of orientation and all planned techniques. On the one hand, the inner pre-run shows you whether you have enough orientation in the cataract, and on the other it gives you an overview of your fear. If you see yourself getting disorientated, ending up in a fat hole or an under cut, then you could be facing a problem.
If the run holds a positive mental image and you do not spend time worrying, then it sits well with you, and you will be motivated to do the rapid.

Motivation

Even if you are mentally prepared (see above), you may still have some worries. If you decide to run it anyway, you must now motivate yourself positively before you start, and not waste time thinking about things that could stop you. Only leave the eddy when you are sure that you will make a clean run of it! You need a strong positive feeling for a successful run – you need to lose the fear!

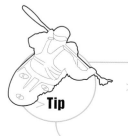

> **Tip** > It's better to regret portaging a section than to regret not portaging it!

Chicken line on the Stikine river, Canada

Tricks

The simplest line

Despite all the hype about "ridin' the main current", it is sometimes simply not possible, and using a side channel keeps you from portaging. In such a situation it is absolutely legitimate to use the so-called "chicken line", because in difficult white water you often have different options for a run, and the main current is not necessarily the best choice. In a border-line situation you should always try to find the safest and the simplest line, which can mean a side channel or in the main current. The simplest line has the most linear and straight forward moves, a linear move having the ad-vantage that you never have to turn your boat across the current. If the technically simplest line is also the safest one, then why shouldn't it also be the most spectacular...?

Fast rolling

Capsizes are common in difficult white water, but with a reliable, fast roll on both sides you will be able to keep even really difficult lines. The most effective and entertaining training for your roll is definitely rodeo paddling.

Plan B

Despite all plans and good intentions, you will screw up a line from time to time. Blessed is he who has an emergency plan or an alternative route. The emergency plan can be either an eddy or another route. Taking the alternative route means having to leave the optimal line, but also involves planning it like the main line: with points of orientation, targets and an inner pre-run.

The V-Drive cataract demands a great deal of courage, or creative portaging. Stikine River, Canada

Epilogue

The fascinating evolution of white water river running will continue as long as the sport exists. New developments will make the adventure of kayaking and experience of nature in white water more attractive and enjoyable in ways that cannot be imagined today. However, even in the future it is likely that revolutionary changes will come in phases. Future generations of white water athletes will carry the sport to realms unimaginable today. In this context one might ask, where are the limits – how far can we go?

Will kayaking techniques and capabilities improve further? Can we as human beings adjust and face even more challenging possibilities? Will there be new materials that enable us to unlock new perspectives? Can we use them to overcome our existing physical limitations?

Steep creek high end

In running waterfalls the limitations are simple. Most importantly, they include the restriction of the human body to absorb impact energy. When you chuck yourself down 80 to 100 foot waterfalls, one does not need to fantasize much to imagine what might happen if something goes wrong.

Every single white water "hero" has hurt himself (or herself) in the past, most of the guys can hardly walk upright after two weeks of serious steep creeking. So, listen to your feelings and inner voice, use your brains, and finally, take specific care of your back. Seal launches from even 10 feet can hurt badly, depending on how you land. The magical limit where risk drastically increases in running waterfalls is still around 30 feet. A general athletic workout, especially concentrating on your torso musculature (abdominals and back), is important for maintaining good body-tension that enables the absorption of impact energy.

Big water high end

When facing nature's raw unleashed power, human existence is insignificant. Competence, capabilities, and a big portion of boldness leads big water experts into the chaos of the most horrendous and monstrous exploding hydraulics. When all goes well, it looks playful and easy, and the kayaker appears to be a magician in the midst of chaos. But he has to beware of making mistakes, or he will quickly become as insignificant as the smallest piece of driftwood and vanish without a trace.

Keep in mind that this can happen on your own home turf in high water conditions too. Big water kayaking is high energy paddling. Always remember that your strength and power, as well as the oxygen in your lungs, are not endless.

Endangered white water

Many of the places that white water river runners love are threatened, especially the streams, creeks and rivers of this world. If you want to be a passionate and engaged white water kayaker, you have to support preservation of nature and become an activist. Demonstrations and protests against stupid and senseless destruction of nature need your support. Do not just be a spectator. Those who look away and make excuses may wake up one day and find there are no rivers left to run.

We are kayakers and belong to the first generation of nature's conservationists. We experience nature, respect and love it, we know about its immense value. It is therefore completely absurd when other conservationists want to drive us and keep us away from rivers with the argument that we are part of the problem. Of course there are fragile river systems in the wilderness, as well as conservation areas where large groups, especially commercial groups, have no right to be. Where there is the threat of banning us from rivers, we have to work toward thoughtful and respectful compromises, and afterwards accept the restriction

and regulation of nature's use for the greater good. We must all recognize there are conservationist aspects in the competing interests of other groups like fishermen or those interested in animal habitat. Kayakers and fishermen can battle together for free flowing rivers, as can be seen now for example in Italy's Sesia Valley in the Piedmont area.

Hydropower – a clean energy?

Hydropower is praised by some as a clean energy, and the World Bank has no problems giving enormous amounts of money for the most absurd projects in developing countries. In these and other situations, the overuse of nature's resources and the negative effects and impact on human beings and even entire ecosystems are regularly misjudged or simply ignored.

In the Alps, mini hydropower plants that destroy remote valleys are still being planned and constructed. Often it is only a small circle of private investors who will profit. The general public, the valley's inhabitants, and tourists suffer from the loss of yet another part of nature. To export energy to larger countries like Germany, nations like Switzerland or Austria sacrifice their own habitat and unique alpine landscapes. This again, is completely absurd. If you use rivers, we ask you to commit your own energy and care to keeping them healthy.

By Markus Schmid and Olli Grau

WW-Philosophy:
literature, concepts and ideas

This book deals with the "new school of modern kayaking" and hopefully will give you a deeper insight into the concepts, ways of thinking, and river philosophies of today's generation of white water river runners. It explains in a practical way how to run rivers successfully in a kayak. Moreover, it is a description of a synchronous state. By this we mean the river is a complete entity, each day on it, each of its bends and rapids, are just one piece of the whole. Likewise, all the prior generations make up the history of river running. Whether the ideas we present will make their way as a philosophy over the course of time, and whether they may develop and last, we can not say for sure. And, some of you may even ask, do we actually need a certain philosophy or ethics on the river?

Kayaking is a relatively young mountain and alpine sport, with a rather modest literary tradition. Until recently there have been no uniform or generally agreed river philosophies or ethics. However, some classical books about the sport describe coherent views of white water kayaking as both experience and adventure in nature.

In the German-speaking alpine scene, Herbert Rittlinger (1909 - 1978) and Walter Frentz (1907 - 2004) for example, represent the very active and productive foldboat literature before World War II, and the pioneer days of white water kayaking as we know it today. Both Rittlinger and Frentz have been members of honour in the Alpine Kayak Club.

The exceptional works of Rittlinger include his expedition reports of solo first descents of the Amazon's tributaries in self-contained, multi-day style (1933, 1938). Another outstanding work is his educational textbook, "Die neue Schule des Kanusports" ("The new school of kayak sport") published in 1950 and updated in 1977.

Walter Frentz's brilliant book "In den Schluchten Europas" ("In the canyons of Europe") was published in 1952, featuring sensational photographic documentation and summarizing an era with the most important accounts of first descents in Europe. Frentz was a photographer and early white water film maker (later propaganda cameraman for the Third Reich) capturing the spirit of early and extreme foldboat white water river-runners before World War II. Among the most remarkable of the first descents and early filmed accounts are those of the Grand Canyon of the Verdon in southern France and the Tara Canyon in Yugoslavia, both accomplished by Frentz and friends in 1932. Frentz was the initiator of the HdK, the German university-circle of kayakers, which were organized independently at different German universities. This concept was later taken up in the formation of the Alpine Kayak Club.

In contemporary literature, English speaking authors such as Bill Mason, Dr. Mike Jones, Richard Bangs, and Whit Deshner are the most prominent. Their work is not weighty, philosophical reading like that of the top-heavy German pedants. The genius sketchings of cartoonists such as the late William Nealy and Alan "Foxy" Fox have also caught new trends and the current river spirit.

Jim Snyder's "Squirtbook"

In 1987, squirtboat guru Jim Snyder published his "Squirtbook". Brilliantly illustrated by William Nealy, it was an educational textbook that became a touchstone of contemporary white water literature and philosophy. The philosophical observations and reflections offered by Snyder are wide-open and tolerant, while also being extraordinarily insightful about the dynamics of the water. Snyder's writing melded a certain ethic together with the physics of white water, such as expressed in his squirt concept "charc in equals charc out", which is legendary among the cognoscenti.

In the book his approach to water and kayaking is ingenious. The intellectual comprehension, identification of squirt concepts, subsequent and successful illustrations of "squirt technique" all are exemplary and bear repeated readings. The squirtboaters are now a highly specialized niche minority, but they have immensely influenced the modern evolution of white water kayaking, both in paddling technique and boat design. In particular, their ideas, techniques, and experimental attitude formed one of the bases of the present rodeo scene. In the course of this revolutionary development, the entire concept of boat design was fundamentally changed. As a result, this made new and improved white water techniques possible.

Dave Manby – archetype of the "Riverbum Concept"

Another milestone is Dave Manby's book, "Many rivers to run", published in 1999. This is a compilation of stories from many of the most marked white water expeditionists, and cultivates the "riverbum concept", namely that of kayakers on their life-mission of whitewater river running and expeditions throughout the world. Years ago Mike Jones characterized Dave as the personification of the riverbum spirit, in the all time whitewater topseller "Canoeing down Everest."

"Dave at twenty one would be the youngest member of the team. He invariably wore pullovers with holes in the elbows and oily, torn jeans. This sloppy dress was intentional – Dave deliberately cultivated a way-out external appearance that only masked his real qualities."

"Well, some people never change!" comments Peter "Green Slime" Knowles, another pioneer riverbum and expeditionary guru. For the last 30 years, Dave has been traveling around the world as a builder and carpenter, organizing expeditions and excursions on the rivers of this planet.

Find your own way...

Anybody who loves to run white water has to decide for themselves how important kayaking should be in their lives, and to find their own way. The riverbum, like the surfbum, can embody an ideal; moving from expedition to expedition, trip to trip, and wave to wave, as long as he is able to keep his head above water, financially speaking. But it is possible to get lost in white water kayaking too. It seems advisable to keep a critical distance to role models and idealistic concepts.

Generally, a broad orientation in the sport is the way to go. White water river running offers a wide spectrum of opportunity and possibilities. Before you get too involved and end up over-specialized, you should experiment and amply sound out the many fields and areas in our sport. In the current globalization and internationalization of white water kayaking, the interdisciplinary paddler will do best, being perfectly prepared for all manner of great adventure. A good role model is the "alpine allrounder", who is an expert in many alpine disciplines, and has overall competence in the mountains, whether he finds himself on water, snow, rock, or ice.

Highly specialized extreme white water kayakers often hasten from river to river wearing blinders. In these times of commercialization there are plenty of idiots on the scene. Today they have already forgotten the name of yesterday's river where they ran the monster waterfall. This is sad. Kayaking is not only a physical act, it is also a path though nature and culture, people and friends, with its own philosophical aspects. Too much specialization can lead to stupidity and narrow-mindedness, even among those who fancy themselves as the "cutting edge."

Doug Ammons: a white water philosopher in his ivory tower

The excesses of commercialization and exploitation of whitewater kayaking's ideals have been sharply criticized by the American solo guru Doug Ammons. His stories and satires skewered the pretension of the so-called "rad-dude scene" of the 90s, personified by such water Gods as Konehead Raddison.

Ammons is a white water philosopher and an individual who takes a strong stand for what he believes in, and holds a special position on the scene. The world class river runner and editor of two psychological journals set a brilliant highlight in modern white water history with his three day solo descent through the Grand Canyon of the Stikine. His 1992 trip represented a deeply personal commitment. As told to one of the authors, his ideal was "to do the hardest thing I could conceive of, in the purest style possible." He has followed this ideal repeatedly in other solo descents, most of which are unknown outside of a small group of peers, as well as doing many other expeditions that are more widely known.

The Ph.D holder and father of five has a universal and interdisciplinary view of the world. His criticism of the hyped excesses and distortions in our sport are dreaded among the protagonists of the scene. Even more so though, he has focused on stories that tell of the inspiration, beauty, and challenges of white water journeys. We are looking forward to his forthcoming book, "The laugh of the water nymph" due in 2004.

"More fun boating" – the Alpine Kayak Club

The Alpine Kayak Club has revolutionized and decisively influenced modern white water kayaking for more than three decades with a simple message – "Mehr Spass am Boot", or simply "more fun boating". This motto was suggested by Holger Machatschek, the AKC's founder and member of honour, as a universal "philosophy". It stood for passionate and committed kayaking, always at the front of the movement, with maximum fun and maximum action. Without compromise, and independent from common club structures, AKC members were passionately devoted to the continuity of development in extreme white water kayaking.

The Alpine Kayak Club has more than 400 members today and is still the largest and most solid international group of extreme alpine white water kayakers world-wide. The broad variety of its members, from all walks of life, has always been a guarantee of the success for this extraordinary group.

Throughout the different phases since its foundation in 1972, the AKC has had a formative influence on the most important developments of our sport. In the pioneer decade of 1972-1982, with new fiberglass laminates, the limits of alpine white water kayaking were newly redefined.

During the first ten years, seven club members had fatal accidents, including one president in office. As a result of these accidents, the ensuing decade (1980-1990), and the years following have seen ongoing discussions about safety in the club. After collecting material among its members, the AKC printed the pioneering safety booklet "Kanu Gefahren", or "Kayaking dangers" in 1985, concisely summarizing basic information about rescue and safety for extreme white water river runners. Unfortunately, despite being copied conceptually into foreign languages, this great little book has never been published on a broader basis in English. Despite what various businesses may claim, or ill-informed, self-proclaimed historians may say, almost every single piece of specialized kayaking equipment for white water safety goes back to the Alpine Kayak Club.

The expeditionary phase and deliberate internationalization of the AKC started in about 1980 and continues today. The radical changes of white water kayaking in our time and its globalization beginning around 1990 were greatly influenced and personified by leading international members of the AKC. The club has been an ongoing movement, and its members have always understood the importance of integrating the world's major white water scenes into its activities. The club's international representatives come from more than 20 countries, and many of the world's best white water river runners are members. As a result, nearly every important expedition and first descent has had at least a few club members participating.

In this context, Holger Machatschek's great programmatic and philosophical achievements for the overall development of international white water sport have not yet been sufficiently described nor acknowledged. Holger, the Alpine Kayak Club's founder and member of honor, stands next to white water legends and pioneers such as Walt Blackadar and Mike Jones.

Philosophies: just words and water

"River philosophies may help you, but they only bring you so far', says Snyder (freely interpreted). "If you don't share them, don't let that get in your way. Philosophies are only words, and it's only water. Half the fun is not knowing what you're doing. The power of the charc is all that matters."

So it just depends on you personally, what you want to do or achieve in white water kayaking, and whether you need a certain philosophy or ethic or not. The most important thing may just be having as much fun as possible.

by Markus Schmid

(translated by Markus Schmid, corrected and re-edited by Doug Ammons)

A last word

Live your dreams

The essence of the "new school of kayaking" in white water is controlled, safe kayaking, which as a consequence means more fun in your boat. With the techniques, tactics, ideas and thoughts introduced here you will be ᵔle to reach the highest spheres of paddling ᵔut being a full-time pro. You just have to what your personal goals are.

ᵔrds of this book are again dedi- ᵔotivate: in white water you have the chance to live your dreams. Keep working at yourself, and try to develop a lifelong interaction between you and the river. It is a wonderful partner, and still holds so many challenges for generations to come. Last but not least, share the fun you have on river with friends – shared fun is twice the fun.

On a wave,

About the author

Water – liquid or frozen – is Olli Grau's element, and for him every day on a wild river or in an untouched powder run is a day in life that should be celebrated. Born on the 31st of July 1974 in Speyer/ Germany he develops his multi-sports talent yet in his early years with gymnastics and basketball. He gains his first freestyle experiences on a BMX-bike, digging his own ramps and jumps, and even broken frames and minor injuries can't stop his enthusiasm. His next piece of equipment is a slalom kayak, but training on a regular basis, performance tests and races are not really Olli's world. He prefers direct competition and the challenge with himself, his closest friends or nature, and therefore he needs no coach or training schedule. A trip to New Zealand sees him then turn his back on slalom competitions for ever, and from then on he works as raft guide, learns to cartwheel in the bottom hole of the Kaituna river, and returns to Germany as a rodeo-grandmaster. The official highlights of his career are the title of the rodeo world champion in 1995, and a run on the Grand Canyon of the Stikine in Canada, which is rated as one of the most difficult kayak trips worldwide. But the simple things in life are as important to Olli as an official title: the publication of his book "Rodeo Boating", a top-to-bottom run of the Inn river or the Raundalselva in Norway, or knee-deep powder in a chute near Chamonix.

But also imparting knowledge plays a major role in Olli's life – he guides extreme white water trips and teaches rodeo paddling. And as a consequence, water – frozen or liquid – will always be Olli's most important element in life.

Bibliography

Educational books

Alpiner Kajak Club
Kanu Gefahren
München, AKC 1987

Baur, Jürgen/Holz Peter
Kanufahren
München, Nymphenburger 1987

Bechdel, Less/Ray, Slim
River Rescue
Boston, Appalachian Mountain Club 1985

Grau, Olli
Richtig Rodeofahren
Raubling, La Ola 1999

Machatschek, Holger
Richtig Wildwasserfahren
München, BLV 1986

Nealy, William
Kayak
Birmingham, Menasha Ridge 1993

Rittlinger, Herbert
Die neue Schule des Kanusports
Leipzig, Brockhaus 1954

Snyder James E./Nealy, William
The Squirt Book
Birmingham, Menasha Ridge 1987

Robert/Pause, Walter
e – Kajakflüsse
., BLV 1969

h des Wassersports I-VI
sport)
rg, Maier 1939

Philosophy

Ammons, Doug
The laugh of the Waternymph
Doug Ammons Waternymph press,
Missoula 2004

Buchheim, Lothar Günther
Tage und Nächte steigen aus dem Strom
Berlin, Fischer 1941

Conrad, Joseph
Das Herz der Finsternis
Frankfurt, Insel Verlag 1992

Deshner, Whit
Does The Wet Suit You?
Seattle, Eddie Tern Press 1981

Deshner, Whit
Travels With A Kayak
Seattle, Eddie Tern Press 1997

Deutscher Kanu Verband
50 Jahre DKV
Hannover 1964

Dickey, James
Flußfahrt
Hamburg 1971, Rowohlt

Fox, "Foxy" Alan
The Blind Probe
Leicester, Cordee 1991

Fox, "Foxy" Alan
The Black Hole
by Alan Francis Fox 1986

Fox, "Foxy" Alan
The Adventures of Boris Surfski
by Alan Francis Fox 1986

Jones, Mike
Sturzfahrt vom Everest
München/Wien, Franz Schneider 1980

Frentz, Walter
In den Schluchten Europas
Stuttgart, Kreuz 1952

Kane, Joe
Running The Amazon
New York, Vintage 1990

Krupski, Ottomar
Vom Triglav zur Adria
Halle, Knapp 1937

Luther, Carl Joseph
Paddelsport und Flußwandern
Stuttgart, Dieck 1923

Manby, Dave
Many Rivers To Run
Dave Manby 1999

Nealy, William
Kayaks To Hell
Hillsborough, Menasha Ridge 1982

Nealy, William
Whitewater Tales Of Terror
Hillsborough, Menasha Ridge 1983

Pawlata, Eddi Hans
Kipp Kipp Hurra
Wien, Pawlata 1928

Pinniger, Deb
L 'eau vive
Deb Pinniger 2003

Simpson, Joe
Touching The Void
London, Random House 1988

Rittlinger, Herbert
Faltboot stößt vor
Leipzig, Brockhaus 1934

Rittlinger, Herbert
Ich kam die reißenden Flüsse herab
Leipzig, Brockhaus 1938

Schwerla, Carl Borro
Kanada im Faltboot
Berlin, August Scherl 1930

Watters, Ron
Never Turn Back
Pocatello, Great Rift Press

Register

paddle **the**
ultimate combination

boats: daggereurope.com
gear: palmequipmenteurope.com
palmequipmentusa.com

image: jed weingarten

147

I wish someone would design a boat that...

Was forgiving to learn in but gives the beginner and intermediate the opportunity to learn how to flat spin and surf in holes.
— Tony Wichy: Four Corners, Durango, CO

Has a performance hull but not designed for the rodeo star. I want a boat that's comfortable and gives me confidence.
— Bob Taylor: Appomattox River Company, Farmville, VA

Doesn't sacrifice speed for play. A boat that can run bigger rapids but still plays well.
— Dale Adams: Beauty Mountain, Fayetteville, WV

That I can surf with and still run class V.
— Jock Bradley: Rippin Productions, Seattle, WA

I just want one boat that I can take anywhere.
— John Hart: Kayak Shed, Hood River, OR

...does it all.

liquidlogic™
[liquidlogickayaks.com]
[liquidlogickayaks.de]

Hoss

Lil' Joe

Hull Detail

THE SUV OF KAYAKS

DIESEL

Made for all conditions. From cruising to creeking to surfing, the Diesel will be the one boat you take everywhere. Designed for maximum comfort, smooth control, mindless stability and surprising speed, the Diesel is a well-rounded performer.

WAVE SPORT

BACK TO THE CORE.

WAVE SPORT
EST. 1986

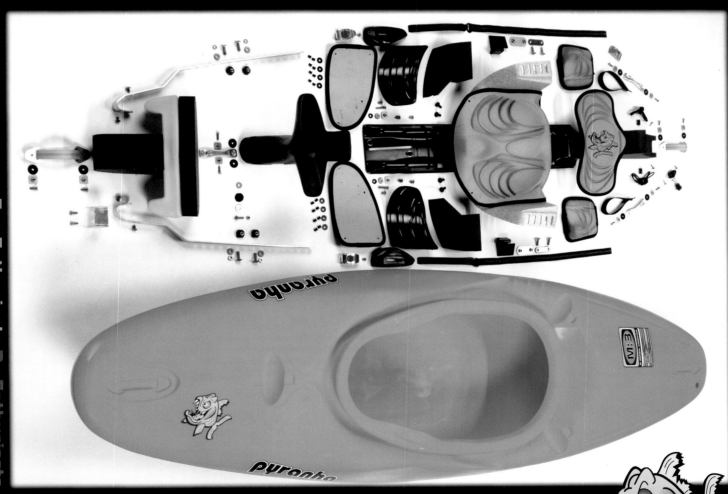

blueandwhite

Soča

Umfangreicher Reise- und Bildband über einen der schönsten Flüsse Europas und das beliebteste Paddelrevier von WW-Kajakfahrern.

Blue And White Kalender 2004

13 Poster sollt ihr sein!

Yukon I

Hervorragend bebilderter und gestalteter Kanuführer vom Traumziel aller Kanadier-paddler. Band I enthält den Yukon, Alsek und Tatshenshini und weitere 10 Flüsse.

Yukon II

Hervorragend bebilderter und gestalteter Kanuführer vom Traumziel aller Kanadier-paddler. Band II enthält den South Naha-ni und weitere 11 Flüsse.

L'Eau Vive

Eine Fotoreise durch die Wasser dieser Welt von Europa über Afrika und Asien bis nach Amerika.

Stikine

Erleben sie eine spannende Expedition auf einem der schönsten und berüchtigs-ten Flüsse Kanadas.

Sick Line III

Spektakuläre Szenen aus den besten WW-Revieren der Erde: Neuseeland, Norwegen und die Alpen. Atemberaubend und schön.

Sick Line I

Der Ursprung! Gefühlvolles Video mit herrlichem Wildwasser aus unserer europäischen Heimat.

Sick Line II

Der Film wurde beim Bergfilmfestival Santander mit dem Preis ausgezeichnet: „Der Film, der am einduckvollsten die Ausübung eines Sports in der Bergwelt dokumentiert."

Young Fresh ‚N' New

New School Video mit den Young Guns der deutschen Paddlerszene. Spielboot-fahren auf heimischen Gefilden und Wild-wasser aus den Alpen und Europa.

Boof Chicken Boof

Olaf Obsommers Regiedebut nimmt uns mit auf eine wundersame Reise. Unter anderem in den Sonnenstaat Kalifornien und auf die Vulkaninsel Reunion.

Richtig Rodeofahren

Ausgezeichnetes Spielboot-Lehrvideo. Die Kunst von Blunts und Catrwheels leicht gemacht!

LANGER
H2O-PROTECTION

Superlight Langarmshirt

Wenn es richtig warm beim Paddeln sein soll, kommt man an Superlight kaum vorbei. Das dünne, extrem flexible Neopren isoliert besser, als es ein Fleecepulli jemals kann. Dazu ist das Material schnelltrocknend und angenehm zu tragen. Die Flatlocknähte stören nicht und Lycraeinsätze unter den Armen verbessern die Bewegungsfreiheit. Einfach unter der Paddeljacke tragen, oder an ganz heißen Tagen auch mal nur mit dem Langarmshirt aufs Wasser gehen.

Long John Dream Herren

Wer den außergewöhnlichen Tragekomfort sucht und auf perfekten Wärmeschutz nicht verzichten will, der hat mit dem Dream das richtige Teil gefunden. Der Dream Long John ist unser Topmodell und meistverkaufter Anzug. Beste Neoprenqualitäten in Verbindung mit einer ausgeklügelten Schnittführung machen den Anzug so angenehm. Das besondere Innenfutter und flexible Einsätze an beanspruchten Stellen sorgen für zusätzlichen Komfort. Den Long John Dream gibt es in 22 Größen!

Superlight Shorts

Superlight Kurzarmshirt

Superlight Hose

Hose Dream

Shorts Dream

Blue And White GmbH
Eichenstraße 3
D 83083 Riedering
Tel.: ++49 8036 90630
info@kajak.de